AN EASY WAY TO

THE UNDERSTANDING of THE QURAN

Part I

Dr. Hasanuddin Ahmed

KITAB BHAVAN
New Delhi-110002

KITAB BHAVAN
Publishers, Distributors, Exporters & Importers
1784, Kalan Maḥal, Darya Ganj,
New Delhi - 1100 02 (India)

Phones : (91-11) 23277392/93, 23274686, 32906494
Fax : (91-11) 23263383
Website : www.kitabbhavan.com
Email : nasri@vsnl.com
: nusrat@bol.net.in

ISBN : 81-7151-100-7 (PB) Set
ISBN : 81-7151-101-5 (Vol. I)

Printed & Published in India by :
Nusrat Ali Nasri for KITAB BHAVAN
1784, Kalan Mahal, Darya Ganj,
New Delhi - 1100 02 [India]

INTRODUCTION

These lists of words from the Quran form part of a significant project started with the aim of creating among the Muslims capability to comprehend the Quran and to cultivate the zest for assimilation of its teachings and philosophy touching on the widest spectrum of life.

THE QURAN

The Quran has been a charter for humanity upwards of fourteen hundred years. Muslims the world over believe in its divine revelation and consider it par excellence the word of Allah. Thus for myriads of Muslims the Quran is a meeting point of belief and brotherhood, the source and mainspring of right thought and action. To Muslims the Quran is not only Code of life but also a source of guidance to humanity at large.

The reason why many Muslims are deprived of the benefits of the Quran is that they think that the Quran is difficult to understand by self effort. The fact is that when the Quran is approached objectively it meets its reader at his own level of comprehension and reveals its meaning to him according to his intellectual capacity.

The Quranic truths have come down to us with pellucid clarity, that its word music and rhythm are in perfect confluence with its meaning and message—this extraordinary symphony of tone and text symbiosis is unique and sinks spontaneously both in head and heart. It is because of this fact that when the Bedouins of Arabia first heard the Quran, they could grasp it. But along with this simplicity the Quran holds a wealth of meaning, for example: the whole of Islamic Law of inheritance is based on a few ayat from Sura 'Al-Nisa' (chapter IV). Although these Ayat are few, they are all embracing in depth and amplitude and form part of Fiqh (Islamic Law), and constitute by themselves a comprehensive legal system. The Quran explains its terms at one place; at another it elucidates them.

The Quran rivets the reader's attention and when one reads it carefully, it influences profoundly. There is only one condition it imposes on the reader that he should read the Quran with an open mind without any reservation. There cannot be a more reasonable condition, for an impartial study.

The word Quran is derived from the word 'Qira' which means to call, to proclaim (the truth). The English word "cry" in a particular context has similar connotational affinity. According to the chronological arrangement of chapters, the first word of the Quran is 'lqra' which is an imperative form of Qira. The meaning of the word 'Iqra' would be to proclaim (the truth) not merely 'read' as is commonly translated. The meaning of the word Quran would be a proclamation, a charter. Moulana Hali has called it 'the voice of the Guide.' Of his lines:

> "Was it the sound of the lightening
> or the voice of the Guide that shook
> the whole land of Arabia? It filled
> the hearts with a new desire. With
> one call all the sleeping people were
> awakened".

That which must have awakened the people from their stupor of ages could not be a written book but a call, a cry from the heart, a message, first uttered and then written down. The Prophet himself had made arrangements for the writing of the Quran and this work was done by Ali bin Abi Talib, Zaid Bin Thabit, Maawia and some others under his personal direction. In this sense the Quran can be considered a collection of revealed oral messages or addresses.

In every country, at all times, the language that is spoken is different from that which is written. The spoken language cannot match the literary written language. The force of the colloquial cannot be retained in the formal niceties of the written language. What is spoken impinges on the moment; its impact and effect cannot be reproduced in the written language. The celestial melody and intrinsic merit of the Quran struck the Arabs dumb when they first heard it as well as when it was written down word by word. This spoken message turned into a masterpiece of literature and the oral messages revealed at intervals became a Code of life for all times. This in itself is a miracle not only for believers in the Book, but also for others since it encompasses fundamental realities. The claim of the Quran to its scriptural divine orgin rests on this plea.

Another point to be considered is that with the passage of time semantic changes take place in languages. Anglo-Saxon was the fore-runner of English language, but English has since become a vastly different language. Even the language of Chaucer (1340-1400) written about 600 years ago can be understood with the aid of linguistic experts. The Urdu speaking people of our day would be hard put to understand the form of Urdu, prevalent five hundred years ago, known as Dakhni. The same is the case with other languages of the world. The exception is Arabic. It should be noted that there is not much difference in the Arabic as it is spoken in the time of the Prophet, and which constitutes the language of the Quran.[1] It is no exaggeration to say that the Arabic language still draws its inspiration and etimological structure from the Quranic prototype. This is due mainly to the influence of the Quran on the Arabic language. Since its revelation, the Quran has retained its syntactic and linguistic supremacy over spoken and written Arabic.

The lapse of 14 centuries reveals no sign of decrease or diminution in the ardent love and fervour the Muslims have for the Quran. On the other hand, as human knowledge in different fields increases the position of the Quran enhances in the esteem of man because the new theories do not conflict with the Quranic views. In fact Quran comprehends them, or corrects them, if there are flaws and short-comings.[2]

1. Dr. Mohd. Hameedullah—Bahavalpur lectures—Islamia University, Pakistan
2. Dr. Mohd. Rafiuddin—Quran Aur Ilme Jadeed. Idarah Sikhafat-e-Islamia, Lahore—Pakistan 1956.

Barring the early period of Islam the possibilities of in-depth study of the Quran were never so bright as they are today. But the reason why we are not able to avail ourselves of these chances is that we do not have an Imam Gazali, or a Moulana Rum or a Dr. Iqbal amongst us who could enable the Muslim mind to imbibe the meaning and the spirit of the Quran.

The Quran has been a meeting point of belief for all Muslims and there has been no change of a single word or syllable in its text. But when we consider the plethora of interpretations and explanations of the Quran, we learn that human incapacity, selfishness and vested interest during fourteen hundred years, have screened and side-tracked the clear and simple teaching of the Book. This involves very important and far reaching results. The Quran had once held aloft the banner of progress for all mankind but unhappily today, its wrong interpretations and faulty explanations have led to the backwardness of the Muslims.

The story of Islam can be thus summed up: Because of the Quran; was the awakening and ascendancy; because of its wrong interpretations the relaps in to backwardness and back-sliding. All was gained because of the Quran; once again high achievement can be attained by means of the Quran only, provided we approach it correctly, assimilate its spirit, understand its teachings, and act in conscientious confirmity. If we so endeavour to understand the Quran the elements covering its real meaning will be removed and we shall be able to see its teaching and tenets in the true light. As Dr. Iqbal has pointed out some of the early Muslim scholars interpreted the Quran in the light of the Greek philosophy. Almost two hundred years later it dawned upon them that the spirit of Islam was totally against this philosophy as well as Greek mythology. Similarly, when the Muslims conquered Persia, the conquerors were influenced by the Persian civilization and philosophy. The Greek and Persian (Ajami) influences, thus adversely affected the interpretation of the Quran relegating it from an open bright book from on high into the arena of a mysterious scripture. Later, learned men from amongst the Muslims felt that these veils should be lifted and Muslims mind should be attuned to the true spirit of Islam. This is possible only when we try to derive the benefit directly from the Quranic text by reading it and understanding it. These developments led to a healthy reaction against both the Greek and Persian (Ajami) influences.

The Quran is the means for making the inner and the outer life of human beings clean and decent and for the betterment of prospects of life in both the worlds, provided we understand and practice its teachings. To know the Quran is to know the destiny of life.

UNDERSTANDING OF THE QURAN

By closing the door of enlightment from the Quran, the Muslims have opened on themselves a hundred windows of misery and trouble. The greatest need for the Muslims today is to create for themselves a capability to understand the Quran. Attempts are being made in the Islamic world to re-discover the Quran in its true light. It would indeed be a great accomplishment of our time if Muslims go back to the Quran as an Infallible guide without which they, as a body, would not be able to play their destined role or discharge their vital responsibilities.

The need of the day is to create and construct a mental orientation, and attitude particularly among the Muslim youth, that is in accord with the aim and purpose of Quranic teachings. To achieve this there can be two ways: one to learn the Arabic language; the other to get acquainted with the teachings of the Quran through the existing translations of the text.

For those students whose mother tongue is not Arabic, it will not be easy to gain proficiency in Arabic while studying their prescribed courses in other languages. The very existence of babel of languages in the world seems to be the will of Allah. In these circumstances, though not impossible to learn Arabic certainly presents difficulties.

LIMITATIONS OF TRANSLATIONS

There are more than ninety translations of the Quran in the Urdu language and more than thirty translations in English. Translations and explanations do go some way to help people understand the meaning of the Quran, but they alone cannot create a capability for comprehension. Translations have their limitations and shortcomings. No matter how successful a translation is, it cannot convey the original sense and feeling and it can never be perfect. The masterpiece of a language cannot be rendered in purity and precision in another language; the nuances of thought and delicate shades of meaning and ideas; depth of feeling and sensitivity of impressions cannot be conveyed with the self-same characteristics of style and diction, as in the original language.

Translations therefore, have this inherent weakness of imperfection. Translations of the Quran suffer from an additional handicap as they represent human efforts to translate the Divine word into other languages.

What is true of translations is equally true of Tafasir (explanations and interpretations). However voluminously they may add to the knowledge about the Quran they cannot provide intimate insight needed.

THE WAY OUT

The Muslims are familiar with the text of the Quran. As in the Salat, five times a day, they recite or listen to the opening chapter - Surah Al - Feteha—and several verses of the Quran in the original Arabic. This extra-ordinary phenomenon is a part of our heritage and we should put it to greater use. Basing on the familiarity with the text if we endeavour to acquire the understanding of the Quran also, it would be a great advantage and we would be on the way to grasping the spirit of the Quran.

For those who do not know Arabic, the most intelligent and scientific way to grasp the spirit and the meaning of the Quran, would be to learn at least those words (with their meaning) which are often repeated in the Quran.

If one wants to gain familiarity with a greater portion of the Quran in as less time as possible, the one way open would be to get acquainted with those words which frequently occur in the Book. This method will prove easier and most useful for students of the Quran.

In other words, it is our responsibility and also the need of the hour to make our younger generation familiar with the Quranic words; the Quranic termninology, and the Quranic proverbs, while we exposc them to the conventional reading of the Quran.

WORD COUNTING

For the present we shall confine ourselves to words only. Oftrepeated words can be remembered by students and retained in mind. It is but appropriate that the term "Word Counting" should be explained here. Word Counting means counting the words of selected pieces of representative literature (of a language) and determining the frequency of words in the corpus. From such counting of words, a frequency list is prepared to indicate that some words are more frequently used while others are not (so frequently used.) The lists of frequently used words are a great asset in learning of a language and its popularization. Word Counting becomes important when on this basis words which occur frequently are carefully selected to be taught to the uninitiated. The learner will be benefitted far more by learning those words whose frequency is ten or more, than learning those words which have been used only once or twice.

For teaching purpose, educationists have accepted the importance of selected vocabulary and have recommended this method.

QURANIC WORD COUNTING

For the purpose of popularizing the understanding of Quran all the words occuring in the Quran are treated as a corpus and from this word frequency is determined.

In the first list of this book 835 words whose frequency in the Quran is ten or more have been selected.

In the second list 976 words which have been used in the Quran five to nine times have been selected.

A word counting of the Arabic language has already been done[1] but this is outside our purview. For the preparation of the aforementioned lists we have taken help from "Al - Mu'Jam al - Mufharas" compiled by Mohd. Fuad Abdul Baqi.

At the initial stage if the students are taught the 835 Quranic words of the first list and then the 976 words of the second list, Insha Allah, the revolutionary methd of teaching the Quran should produce striking results.

The need for the study of selected words arises out of practical considerations of which the foremost is the time factor. The time at the disposal of the student for the study of the Quran in Arabic, a foreign language is in most cases very limited. It is, therefore, evident that the Quranic words to be taught in the first instance should be selected ones, so that by learning fewer words one may be able to master greater portion of the text of the Quran.

It is clear that the realm of the Quran with its magnificence is made up of words. A knowledge of the vocabulary of the Quran is, therefore, a pre-requisite for the knowledge and understanding of the Quran and subsequently of its higher values.

It is necessary to clarify that by Quranic words we mean all those derivations as they occur in the Quran. Each derivative as it occurs in the Book is taken as a word and not its origin or root. Thus in these lists every derived word from

1. The basic word list of the Arabic Daily Newspaper compiled by Moshe Brille, the Hebrew University Press Association, Jerusalam 1940.

the root and not the root itself, has been counted as a word. Had only the root been made the basis, the number of the words would have been considerably reduced. It would then be necessary to acquaint the students with all the derived forms of an origin and point out particularly those words which have frequently been used in the Quran. This work can be done only by trained teachers. In the project of which these lists are a part, counting of Quranic words on the basis of the root, has also been started. When these lists are prepared, there will be instructions for the teachers as well. The present lists of frequently used words of the Quran can be used by the students without the help of a trained teacher.

According to the present approach (and of Al Mu'jam al Mufharas) there are 11742 different derivations or words out of which:

1. 6579 are derivations or words whose frequency in the Quran is one.
2. 3352 are derivations or words whose frequency in the Quran is two to four. The total occurrence is 8621.
3. 976 are derivations or words whose frequency in the Quran is five to nine. The total occurrence is 6258.
4. 835 are derivations or words whose frequency in the Quran is ten or more. The total occurrence is 30312.

Derivations or words mentioned against number 4 and 3 have been included in the 1st and the 2nd lists respectively. The total number of the above 11742 derivations or words from the Quran, on the basis of frequency is 51770.

As is clear from the above chart, a student who is taught the 835 words of the first list will get acquainted with 58.63% of the text. A student who is acquainted with the 1811 words of the 1st and 2nd list will get acquainted with 70.64% of the text

It stands to reason that the easier we make it for the pupil to learn the mechanical and technical aspects of the language, the easier it will be for him to get initiated into the true spirit of the Quran. Moreover he will have the advantage of the direct access to the original words.

The knowledge to a student that the acquisition of 835 specific words would enable him to understand approximately 60% of the words he meets in the Quran would certainly act as a valuable stimulus for further progress.

QURANIC TERMS

So far, we have been talking only about the words, but besides the words there are terms and representative words used in the Quran, which have a terminology of their own.

There are many words which have been used in some special sense quite different from their ordinary connotation. It is imperative to know these terms and the representative words if one wants to grasp the essence of the Quran.

If a word is used in a special sense, and if it pertains to any discipline of letters, it is called a term. Terms are in reality hints which turn the mind towards the cluster (group) of thoughts and ideas they contain. Just as letters are necessary for words, and words are required to make up sentences, in the same manner terms are inevitable for any discipline. For every art or discipline, and for every philosophy or idealism, there are particular terms through which the meaning and connotations are explained and elucidated. Iqbal proclaimed a new message through his poetry, likewise, he had to use a particular terminology for it. One of the famous terms is 'Khudi' - ego. Unless we understand these terms we cannot fully grasp the message in Iqbal's poetry. The Quran is pre-eminently 'Al Hikmat' - a Book of Wisdom—and in it not less than 37 terms have been used.

In order to understand the Quran a clear comprehension of the full connotation of these terms is a sine qua non. In the beginning the Prophet of Islam (PBUH) himself explained these terms to his followers, but in later centuries their real meaning slipped from the Muslim mind and changes crept in. Thus every term was expanded in its connotation and became elastic to accommodate the new trends of thought relating to that term.*

When the Quran was translated, they tried to translate along with words the terms also and little attention was paid to bring out the sense in which they were used. For example the term Salat has been translated in English as prayer, worship etc, and namaz in Urdu and so on.

As mentioned earlier, it is one of the merits of the Quran that it explains and elucidates its own terms. As such, any attempt to translate the terms or to find equivalents is undesirable, if not futile. Whichever the language into which the Quran is being translated or explained, the terminology should be left untampered.

REPRESENTATIVE WORDS OF THE QURAN

The difference between the general words and representative words of the Quran should also be maintained. For every revolutionary movement representative words are important because it is through them that the fundamental principles of the message are explained. The Quran has also used its represenative words to spread its message.

The lists of 37 terms and 62 representative words of the Quran are included as appendices.

QURANIC PROVERBS

Every word of the Quran is like a gem set in its proper place. Any replacement, change, or displacement cannot but detract from the brilliance of the syntax, not to mention irreparable damage to the immaculately integrated conception. In every line of the Quran lie treasures of latent wisdom, and there are about 500 proverbs which contain high ideals and rare beauty of elevated thought expressing in a few words the quintesence of Quranic teachings. These

* Maulana Maududi in his introduction to "The Four Basic Terms of the Quran" has also expressed similar views.

proverbs are landmarks and to get acquainted with them is to acquire inner access to the Quran itself. To know the Quran one must know them. By way of illustration only 21 of these proverbs along with their meaning (in English) have been included in this publication.

THE PROJECT

We have now under preparation, part II consisting of the 37 Quranic terms, 62 representative words of the Quran with explanatory notes and 500 Quranic proverbs with translations in English. The second part will be published as the second phase of the project.

The project of which this presentation is a part is first of its kind. It is experimental in nature. It cannot claim perfection. If others follow where I have in my own humble way made a start, I will be amply rewarded.

I am fully aware of my own limitations and of the shortcomings of the present edition. Suggestions for improvements will always be welcome.

ACKNOWLEDGEMENTS

I extend my deepest thanks to my good friend Mr. Iqbal Alladin of Hyderabad, India for the keen interest taken in the project in its initial and crucial stage.

I also thank my son Mr. Zaheer Ahmed for the comfort and facilities provided with great care and devotion which enabled me to complete this book in spite of the present condition of my health. May Allah reward him.

The Urdu edition was published in India in February 1986, in which the English equivalents for the Quranic words were provided side by side the Urdu equivalents. Before publication of the present edition the work has been thoroughly scrutinized word by word. It was then revised by Dr. Ahmad H. Sakr whose mother tongue is Arabic and who is one of the great authorities on the subject in this part of the world. The real source of his contribution, however, was his genuine and pious interest. Sincere thanks are therefore, due to him.

I hope this English edition which is being published by the Iqra International Educational Foundation as a result of the personal interest evinced by its dynamic Secretary Mr. Mohammad Mazhar Hussaini, will get a positive response and will herald editions in other languages.

It is my earnest prayer that Allah will accept this humble effort and make it useful for an easy understanding of the Quran.

November 25, 1986 Dr. Hasanuddin Ahmed

2528 Brunswick Cr.,
Woodridge, IL 60517, U.S.A.

PART ONE

A List of 835 Words of the Quran whose frequency in the Quran is 10 and above

with meanings in English

By knowing the words one can understand 58.63 percent text of the Quran

NOTE: In both lists the terms and the representative words of the Quran (along with derivitives) have been given asterisks and stars respectively. Explanatory notes on the terms and the representative words of the Quran are given in the second part.

1	Forever, Never	أَبَدًا
2	Ibrahim, name of Prophet	إِبْرٰهِم
3	To his father	لِأَبِيْهِ
4	Our fathers (dir. obj.)	اٰبَآءَنَا
5	Your fathers (pl)	اٰبَآؤُكُمْ
6	Our fathers (subj)	اٰبَآؤُنَا
7	(You) commit, you come (pl)	تَأْتُوْنَ
8	She/it comes to them, or will come	تَأْتِيَهُمْ
9	(He) brings, comes or will bring	يَأْتِ
10	(He) comes or will come	يَأْتِيَ
11	Reaches them or will reach them	يَأْتِيَهُمْ
12	Come or bring	ائْتُوا
13	He gave them	اٰتٰهُمُ
14	(We) gave	اٰتَيْنَا
15	(We) gave him	اٰتَيْنٰهُ

16	We gave them	اٰتَيْنٰهُم
17	You give (imp) (pl)	اٰتُوا
18	They were given	اُوْتُوا
19	He was given	اُوْتِيَ
20	Sin (subj)	اِثْمٌ
21	Sin (dir. obj)	اِثْمًا
22	Wage, reward	اَجْرٌ
23	Reward (dir. obj)	اَجْرًا
24	Their reward, their wages (subj)	اَجْرُهُمْ
25	Fixed period, yes	اَجَلٌ
26	One, any	اَحَدًا
27	Anybody, somebody, (subj)	اَحَدٌ
28	He caught, he took	اَخَذَ
29	Seized them	اَخَذَتْهُم
30	We took, we caught	اَخَذْنَا
31	(He) has taken, caught	اِتَّخَذَ

32	They took, they adopted	اِتَّخَذُوا
33	You adopted (pl)	تَتَّخِذُوٓا
34	Do not adopt, do not catch	لَا تَتَّخِذُوا
35	Take, render, take to them	يَتَّخِذ
36	The other	الْاٰخَر
37	Others (ind. obj)	اٰخَرِيْنَ
38	Other, also, another	اُخْرٰى
39	Next, following, coming, the last	الْاٰخِر
40	Next, following, coming, the last ones (pl) (ind. obj)	اَلْاٰخِرِيْنَ
41	The here after	اِلْاٰخِرَة
42	His brother (ind. obj)	اَخِيْهِ
43	Adam, name of prophet	اٰدَم
44	Command, permission,	بِاِذْنِ
45	With his permission	بِاِذْنِهٖ

46	The earth (subj. ind. obj)	اَلاَرْض
47	The name of prophet Yacoub	إِسْرَآءِيْل
48	Ismail, name of prophet, son of Ibrahim	إِسْمٰعِيْل
49	Eat (imp) (pl)	تَاْكُلُوا
50	You eat or will eat (pl)	تَاْكُلُوْنَ
51	They eat	يَاْكُلُوْنَ
52	You eat (imp) (pl)	كُلُوْا
53	Those women who	اَلّٰتِيْ
54	Painful (subj), grievous, hurting	اَلِيْم
55	Painful (dir. obj) grievous, hurting	اَلِيْما
56	Object of worship, god (subj) (indir. obj)	اِلٰه
57	god, object of worship (dir. obj.)	اِلٰهاً

58	Your (pl) god, lord	* إِلٰهُكُمْ
59	gods	* آلِهَةً
60	Allah, the only one God	اَللّٰهُ
61	Bounties, benefits, blessings	آلَآءِ
62	I, (We) commanded, instructed, commissioned, entrusted	أُمِرْتُ
63	The command, the affairs, the authority, the decree, the order	اَلْأَمْرِ
64	Command, affair (obj.)	أَمْرًا
65	Our Command, our affair (ind. obj,	أَمْرِنَا
66	His command, his affair (subj)	أَمْرُهٗ
67	Their command, their affair (subj)	أَمْرُهُمْ
68	The commands, the affairs	اَلْأُمُوْرُ
69	His mother, his abode, his origin, his source (dir. obj)	★ أُمَّهٗ

70	People (Ummat), nation, generation	★ أُمَّة
71	Peoples, nations, generations	★ أُمَم
72	He adopted faith, he believed	* اٰمَنَ
73	You (pl) adopted faith	* اٰمَنْتُمْ
74	We professed faith	* اٰمَنَّا
75	They adopted faith	* اٰمَنُوْا
76	Adopt, (imp) faith, (pl)	* تُؤْمِنُوْآ
77	We adopt faith or will adopt	* نُؤْمِنُ
78	He adopts faith or will adopt	* يُؤْمِنُ
79	They adopt faith or will adopt	* يُؤْمِنُوْا
80	They will adopt faith, or will adopt	* يُؤْمِنُوْنَ
81	You adopt faith (imp)	* اٰمِنُوْا
82	Trustworthy, faithful, reliable	* آمِيْن
83	The faith	* اَلْاِيْمَان

84	One who adopted faith	* مُؤْمِن
85	Those who adopted faith (subj)	* مُؤْمِنُوْنَ
86	Those who adopted faith (obj)	* مُؤْمِنِيْنَ
87	The women who adopted faith, the believing women	* اَلْمُؤْمِنٰت
88	Female	اُنْثٰى
89	The human being, mankind human race	اَلْاِنْس
90	The human being	اَلْاِنْسَان
91	As per wish, where from, where, how	اَنّٰى
92	People of (such as people of book)	اَهْل
93	People of (his) household	اَهْلَهٗ
94	People of (her) household	اَهْلِهَا
95	People, descendants, family members	اٰل

96	First	اَوَّل
97	The ancients, the first, the ancestors, the forebearers	اَلْاَوَّلِيْنَ
98	The former (fem)	اَلْاُوْلٰى
99	Possessors of, owners of, the ones with, (subj)	اُوْلُوا
100	Possessors of, owners of, (obj.)	اُوْلِي
101	Their abode, their lodge, their accomodation	مَاْوٰىهُمْ
102	Sign, sentence of the Quran, verse, miracle	اٰيَة
103	Signs, sentence of the Quran, verse, miracles	اٰيٰت
104	Our signs, our miracles, our sentences	اٰيٰتِنَا
105	His signs, his miracles, his sentences	اٰيٰتِهٖ
106	My signs, miracles, my sentences	اٰيٰتِيْ

107	Where, wither	أَيْنَ
108	Which	أَيُّ
109	O, you who. . .	يَاَيُّهَا
110	Our distress, strength, fortitude, courage	بَأْسُنَا
111	How bad, miserable to feign misery or distress	بِئْسَ
112	The ocean, the sea	اَلْبَحْرُ
113	The land, mainland	اَلْبَرّ
114	Increases, to extend	يَبْصُطُ
115	Give good tiding (imp) (sing)	بَشِّرْ
116	Good tidings, good news	بُشْرٰى
117	Man, human being, mankind (ind. obj/subj)	بَشَرٌ
118	Man, human being, mankind (dir. obj)	بَشَرًا
119	They see, look, realize understand, comprehend	يُبْصِرُوْنَ

120	One who sees, understands, realizes, comprehends (subj)	بَصِيْر
121	One who sees, understands, comprehends (obj)	بَصِيْرًا
122	The sights, the insights, perceptions, the visions	اَلْاَبْصَارُ
123	Their eyes (obj)	اَبْصَارِهِمْ
124	The false, the futile, the baseless	★ اَلْبَاطِل
125	Far form, far reaching, unusual, far away, remote	بَعِيْد
126	After, in addition to, beside	بَعْد
127	Thereafter, after that	بَعْدِهٖ
128	After them	بَعْدِهِمْ
129	Some, a little part, portion, a few, some of	بَعْض
130	Some of you	بَعْضُكُمْ
131	Some of them	بَعْضُهُمْ
132	All of a sudden, surprise	بَغْتَةً

133	(If) you (pl) like, wish, desire	تَبْتَغُوا
134	Favour, desire, wish, for the purpose of	اِبْتِغَآء
135	Satan, devil	اِبْلِيْس
136	Reached, attained, (communication)	بَلَغَ ★
137	The communication, the announcement, the proclamation	اَلْبَلٰغ ★
138	Yes, why not, yes, indeed	بَلٰى
139	Son, descendant, offspring	اِبْن
140	Sons, children	بَنِيْ
141	Sons, children, descendants	بَنِيْن
142	Daughters, girls	بَنٰت
143	The door, the entrance	اَلْبَاب
144	Doors, entrances	اَبْوَاب
145	The house, the dwelling place	اَلْبَيْت

146	The houses	اَلْبُيُوْت
147	He indicates, he makes it clear, plain, obvious, or will indicate	يُبَيِّنُ
148	Which indicates, describes, or found out	تَبَيَّنَ
149	Proof, sign, clear evidence	بَيِّنَة
150	The proofs, the signs	اَلْبَيِّنٰت
151	Clear, open. plain, evident, obvious	مُبِيْنٌ
152	Clear, open, obvious (obj)	مُّبِيْنًا
153	In between, among	بَيْنَ
154	Among you (pl)	بَيْنَكُمْ
155	Among us	بَيْنَنَا
156	Among them	بَيْنَهُمْ
157	Between the two	بَيْنَهُمَا
158	Between (you and) me	بَيْنِيْ
159	Followed	اِتَّبَعَ ★

160	They followed	اِتَّبَعُوْا	★
161	They follow or will follow	يَتَّبِعُوْنَ	★
162	Beneath it, (fem)	تَحْتِهَا	
163	(He) left	تَرَكَ	
164	That (fem.)	تِلْكَ	
165	Are recited	تُتْلٰى	*
166	Repented, turned from (in repentance)	تَابَ	★
167	They repented	تَابُوْا	★
168	He turns from or will turn to God's grace	يَتُوْبُ	★
169	The Torah book revealed on prophet Musa	اَلتَّوْرٰىةُ	
170	Three	ثَلٰثَةَ	
171	Followers of Prophet Salih	ثَمُوْدَ	
172	The fruits	اَلثَّمَرٰتِ	
173	Price, reward	ثَمَنًا	
174	Two	اِثْنَيْنِ	

175	The mountains	اَلْجِبَال	
176	The hell, the hellfire, the fire	اَلْجَحِيْم	
177	The criminals	اَلْمُجْرِمُوْن	
178	The criminals (obj)	اَلْمُجْرِمِيْن	
179	To flow, to float, to run, to blow (wind)	تَجْرِيْ	
180	We reward or we will reward	نَجْزِيْ	★
181	He rewards or he will reward	يَجْزِيْ	★
182	Reward, repay	جَزَآء	★
183	He made	جَعَلَ	
184	We made	جَعَلْنَا	
185	We made him	جَعَلْنٰهُ	
186	We made them	جَعَلْنٰهُمْ	
187	They made	جَعَلُوْا	
188	We make	نَجْعَلُ	
189	He makes or he will make	يَجْعَلُ	

190	Make (imp) (sing)	اِجْعَلْ	
191	All, altogether, all of them, entirely, totally	جَمِيعًا	
192	All,	أَجْمَعِينَ	
193	Prohibition, accountability, sin, misdemeanor	جُنَاحٌ	
194	The Ginn	اَلْجِنُّ	
195	The Ginn, the obsession, the insanity	اَلْجِنَّةُ	
196	Mad, lunatic	مَجْنُونٌ	
197	The paradise, the heaven	اَلْجَنَّةُ	★
198	Gardens, heavens	جَنّٰتٌ	
199	They struggled, strived	جٰهَدُوا	*
200	Hell	جَهَنَّمُ	
201	Came, brought	جَآءَ	
202	(She) came	جَآءَتْ	
203	Came to them, reached them	جَآءَتْهُمْ	
204	Came to you	جَآءَكَ	

205	Came to you (pl)	جَآءَكُمْ	
206	Came to them	جَآءَهُمْ	
207	He likes or he will like	يُحِبُّ	
208	The stones, the rocks	اَلْحِجَارَةُ	
209	Talk, speech, chat	حَدِيْث	*
210	Limitations, borders, borderline	حُدُوْدُ	
211	Field or agricultural farm, tilling, tilth	حَرْث	
212	Pain, compulsion, inconvenience, sin	حَرَج	
213	Prohibited	حَرَّمَ	*
214	The respectable, the holy, the forbidden, the sacred	اَلْحَرَامِ	*
215	The parties, the groups	اَلْاَحْزَاب	
216	They grieve, sadden or will grieve	يَحْزَنُوْنَ	
217	Account, reckoning	حِسَاب	*
218	Good, better, well, splendidly, beautifully	حَسَنًا	*

219	Goodness, virtue, good deed charity, benefaction	* حَسَنَةٌ
220	The goodness, the virtue, the best outcome, (fem)	* اَلْحُسْنٰى
221	Best, better, nicer	* اَحْسَنُ
222	The benefactors, the virtuous, the benevolents (obj.)	* اَلْمُحْسِنِيْنَ
223	Came true, verified, correct, be incumbent, deserved it, (punishment)	★ حَقَّ
224	The truth, the true, the right, (correct)	★ اَلْحَق
225	True, genuine, (obj)	★ حَقًّا
226	More deserving, worthiness, more entitled	★ اَحَقُّ
227	He orders, or he will order he passes an opinion	يَحْكُمُ
228	Wisdom, the legal decision, judgement, verdict, jurisdiction	اَلْحُكْمُ
229	The wisdom	★ اَلْحِكْمَةَ
230	Wise, ever-wise	★ حَكِيْم

231	Ever-wise (obj.)	★ حَكِيْمًا
232	They swear, they take oath	يَحْلِفُوْنَ
233	Patient, clement, gentle	حَلِيْم
234	The praise, the command, the thanks	* اَلْحَمْدُ
235	Praise worthy, deserving obedience	* حَمِيْد
236	Hot, boiling, intimate, close	حَمِيْم
237	Unconcerned, straight forward, true behavior (obj)	حَنِيْفًا
238	Where, wherever	حَيْثُ
239	When at the time of, during	حِيْنَ
240	He gives life or he will give life	يُحْيِي
241	The immortal, the alive	اَلْحَيّ
242	The life, the existence	اَلْحَيٰوة
243	Watchful, knower, well-acquaintted	خَبِيْر
244	Watchful, knower, well-acquainted, (obj)	خَبِيْرًا

245	Comes out or will come out, emerges from, flows out	يَخْرُجُ
246	(He) produces, removes, brings before public, or he will produce	أَخْرَجَ
247	He extracts, or will extract	يُخْرِجُ
248	Disgrace, defamacy, shame, dishonor	خِزْيٌ
249	The losers, the perishers (subj)	اَلْخٰسِرُوْنَ
250	The losers, the perishers (obj)	اَلْخٰسِرِيْنَ
251	Permanent dwellers, ever-lasting, eternity (subj)	خٰلِدُوْنَ
252	Permanent dwellers, ever-lasting, eternity (obj)	خٰلِدِيْنَ
253	They differed, disagreed, they opposed	اِخْتَلَفُوْا
254	They differ, disagree, or will differ	يَخْتَلِفُوْنَ
255	Things behind them, successors, descendants, offsprings	خَلْفَهُمْ

256	Created, originated	خَلَقَ
257	He created you (pl)	خَلَقَكُمْ
258	We created	خَلَقْنَا
259	He creates or will create	يَخْلُقُ
260	Creation, creatures, people mankind	خَلْق
261	Passed away, elapsed	خَلَتْ
262	I fear (I am afraid) or I will fear	اَخَاف
263	They fear or will fear	يَخَافُوْنَ
264	Fear, dread, frightening	خَوْف
265	Good, virtuous, better, superior (subj)	خَيْر
266	Good, virtuous, better superior (obj)	خَيْرًا
267	The good deeds, the virtues	اَلْخَيْرٰت
268	Animal of the earth, beast	دَآبَّة
269	They entered, got in, penetrated	دَخَلُوا

270	You enter (imp) (pl)	اُدْخُلُوْا
271	Grades, levels, stages, degrees, ranks	دَرَجٰت
272	Explained to you, comprehended, perceived (sing)	اَدْرٰكَ
273	(pl) You call upon, or you will call, summon, invite	تَدْعُوْنَ
274	They call upon or will call they invite or will invite	يَدْعُوْنَ
275	Call or pray (imp)	اُدْعُ
276	Call or pray (imp) (pl)	اُدْعُوْا
277	Prayer, supplication	دُعَآء
278	Inferior, lower down, (place) nearer, closer	اَدْنٰى
279	The world, the earth	اَلدُّنْيَا
280	The house, the dwelling place, the abode the residence	اَلدَّار
281	Their houses (obj)	دِيَارِهِمْ
282	Except, aside, inferior, below, under	دُوْنِ

283	Except him, other than him, without him, below him, under him	دُوْنِهٖ	
284	The (Din) religion	اَلدِّيْنُ	*
285	Your (Din) religion (pl)	دِيْنِكُمْ	*
286	Their (Din) religion	دِيْنِهِمْ	*
287	Race, descendants, clan, offspring	ذُرِّيَّةً	
288	Remember, bear in mind, think of, keep in mind	اُذْكُرْ	★
289	Remember (imp) (pl) same as before	اُذْكُرُوْا	★
290	You (pl) contemplate or will contemplate, remember, recollect	تَذَكَّرُوْنَ	★
291	(Zikr), recollection, remembrance (subj)	ذِكْرٌ	★
292	(Zikr), recollection rememberance (obj)	ذِكْرًا	★
293	(Zikr), advice, remembrance, (to give) lesson, recollection	ذِكْرٰى	★
294	Masculine, man	ذَكَرٌ	

295	Their sins, mistakes, crimes, misdeeds	ذُنُوبِهِمْ
296	possessor or holder of, endowed with	ذُو
297	Possessor or holder of, endowed with (obj)	ذَا
298	Possessor or holder of (indir. obj.)	ذِى
299	Possessor or holder of (fem) self	ذَاتَ
300	Taste (imp) (pl)	ذُوقُوا
301	Kind, merciful, gracious	رَءُوفٌ
302	He saw, perceived, noticed	رَأَى
303	They saw, noticed	رَأَوْا
304	(You) saw (sing)	رَأَيْتَ
305	I saw	رَأَيْتُ
306	Did you see? (pl) noticed, find out	أَرَءَيْتُمْ
307	You (sing) see or will see (cond)	تَرَ

308	You (sing) see or will see	تَرَىٰ	
309	They will see or will see	يَرَوْا	
310	God (Rubb), lord	رَبِّ	*
311	My lord, God (Rubb)	رَبِّي	*
312	Your (sing) lord, God (Rubb)	رَبُّكَ	*
313	Your (pl) lord, God (Rubb)	رَبِّكُمْ	*
314	Lord (of) both of you	رَبُّكُمَا	*
315	Our lord, God (Rubb)	رَبَّنَآ	*
316	His God, lord (Rubb)	رَبِّهِۦ	*
317	Their God, lord (Rubb)	رَبِّهِمْ	*
318	My lord, God (Rubb)	رَبِّيْ	*
319	They return or will return	يَرْجِعُونَ	
320	You will be returned	تُرْجَعُونَ	
321	Your returning place, retreat, place of refuge, recourse	مَرْجِعُكُمْ	
322	Man	رَجُل	

323	The men	اَلرِّجَال
324	They hope or will hope they wish, they look forward	يَرْجُوْنَ
325	Motherly Love, grace, mercy	رَحْمَة
326	His grace, his mercy (obj)	رَحْمَتِهٖ
327	The most compassionate, merciful	اَلرَّحْمٰن
328	The ever-merciful	اَلرَّحِيْم
329	In a state of ever-merciful, ever-merciful	رَحِيْمًا
330	We gave them (food, etc.), provided, bestowed	رَزَقْنٰهُمْ
331	The food, the provisions, the livelihood, the nourishment	اَلرِّزْق
332	Food, provisions, nourishment (obj)	رِزْقًا
333	We sent, assigned, delegated	* اَرْسَلْنَآ
334	We sent you (sing), delegated you, assigned you	* اَرْسَلْنٰكَ
335	He sends or will send	* يُرْسِلُ

336	Messenger (of Allah) (Rasul) (subj)	رَسُوْلٌ	*
337	Messenger of Allah, (Rasul) (obj)	رَسُوْلًا	*
338	His (Rasul) Messenger	رَسُوْلُهٗ	*
339	The Messengers	اَلرُّسُل	*
340	The Messengers (obj)	رُسُلًا	*
341	Our Messenger (Rasul)	رُسُلُنَا	*
342	His Messengers (Rasul) (indir. obj)	رُسُلِهٖ	*
343	Their Messengers (Rasul)	رُسُلُهُمْ	*
344	The Messengers of Allah, The deputed ones	اَلْمُرْسَلِيْن	*
345	Air, breeze, wind	رِيْح	
346	Air (pl) breezes	اَلرِّيْح	
347	He intended, wished, desired	اَرَادَ	
348	He intends, wishes, or will intend	يُرِيْد	

349	They intend or will intend, wish, desire	يُرِيدُونَ
350	Doubt, suspicion, uncertainty	رَيْبَ
351	The (Zakat) the alms-giving	الزَّكٰوةَ *
352	Wives, pairs, couples (obj) mates, partners	اَزْوَاج
353	Wives, pairs, couples (obj)	اَزْوَاجًا
354	Their wives	اَزْوَاجِهِمْ
355	Was adorned, was decorated	زُيِّنَ
356	Ornament, decoration, attire	زِيْنَةَ
357	I question you or will question you	اَسْئَلُكُمْ
358	They ask you or will ask you	يَسْئَلُوْنَكَ
359	Praise, obey, glorify (imp. sing)	سَبِّحْ *
360	Who is much praised, who is much obeyed	سُبْحٰنَ *
361	Glory be to Him	سُبْحٰنَهٗ *

362	Seven	سَبْعٌ
363	Path, way, road, means, access, public fountain	سَبِيْلٌ
364	Path, way, road, means, access, public fountain (obj)	سَبِيْلًا
365	His path	سَبِيْلِهٖ
366	Those who prostrate in worship	اَلسّٰجِدِيْنَ
367	While prostrating	سُجَّدًا
368	Mosque, place of prostration for worship	مَسْجِد
369	Magic, bewitchment, fascination	سِحْرٌ
370	Magician, sorcerer, wizard	سٰحِر
371	Subjected, exploited	سَخَّرَ
372	One who hastens, quick, prompt, fast	سَرِيْع
373	Extravagants, prodigals, one who exceeds limits (pl, obj)	مُسْرِفِيْنَ

374	Poor (pl), miserable, submissive, beggars	مَسٰكِيْن	
375	Argument, example, representative, authority, power, might, ruler	سُلْطٰن	
376	Argument, example, representative, ruler (obj)	سُلْطٰنًا	
377	Peace, safety, security greeting, salutation	سَلٰم	*
378	Those who accepted Islam, Muslims (subj)	مُسْلِمُوْنَ	*
379	Those who accepted Islam, Muslims (obj)	مُسْلِمِيْنَ	*
380	We heard, listened	سَمِعْنَا	
381	They hear or will hear	يَسْمَعُوْنَ	
382	The hearing, the sense of hearing	اَلسَّمْع	
383	One who hears, ever-hearing, ever-listening	سَمِيْع	
384	Appointed time, fixed time, named, called	مُسَمًّى	

385	Name, noun, reputation	اِسْم
386	The sky, the heaven	اَلسَّمَآء
387	The skies, the heavens	اَلسَّمٰوٰت
388	Way, habit, tradition	سُنَّت
389	Years	سِنِيْنَ
390	Done wrong, bad, wicked	سَآءَ
391	The bad, the evil	اَلسُّوْٓء
392	The evil, the bad, the misdeed	اَلسَّيِّئَة
393	The evils, the misdeeds	اَلسَّيِّاٰت
394	The time, the hour (of judgement), the watch, the clock	اَلسَّاعَة
395	Soon, to put off, you will see	سَوْفَ
396	Became equal, turned to, mounted, established	اِسْتَوٰے
397	To be equal, to be alike	يَسْتَوِيْ
398	Equal, equality, sameness	سَوَآء

399	The tree (the tree of zaqqum)	اَلشَّجَرَة
400	Severe, ever forceful	شَدِيْد
401	Severe, ever forceful (obj)	شَدِيْدًا
402	More severe, more forceful, stronger, harder	اَشَدّ
403	The bad, the evil, the mischief, the calamity	اَلشَّرُّ
404	They joined gods with Allah	* اَشْرَكُوْا
405	They join gods with Allah or will join	* يُشْرِكُوْنَ
406	Partners, associates, companions	* شُرَكَآء
407	Those who join (gods with Allah) (obj)	* اَلْمُشْرِكِيْن
408	The shaitan, the satan, the one who is thrown at distance, the outcast	★ اَلشَّيْطٰن
409	The satans, the devils	★ اَلشَّيٰطِيْن

410	(They) perceive, or will perceive, know, feel, realize, notice	يَشْعُرُونَ
411	Intercession, mediation, advocacy	* شَفَاعَة
412	(You) thank or will thank	تَشْكُرُونَ
413	Doubt, uncertainly, suspicion, misgiving	شَكّ
414	The sun	اَلشَّمْسُ
415	Witness, martyr	★ شَهِيْد
416	Witness (obj)	★ شَهِيْدًا
417	Witnesses, martyrs	★ شُهَدَآء
418	The testimony, the martyrdom	★ اَلشَّهَادَة
419	The month	اَلشَّهْر
420	(He) willed, pleased	شَآءَ
421	We wish or will wish	نَشَآء
422	He wishes or he will wish	يَشَآءُ
423	He wishes or will wish	يَشَاء

424	Thing	شَيْءٌ	
425	Thing (obj)	شَيْئًا	
426	They became, they entered, into morning	اَصْبَحُوْا	
427	They patiently bore, endured	صَبَرُوْا	★
428	Be patien (imp, sing)	اِصْبِرْ	★
429	Those who bear with patience, forebearer (obj)	اَلصّٰبِرِيْن	★
430	Comrade, people, companions of the Prophet	اَصْحٰب	
431	The chests	اَلصُّدُوْر	
432	Their chests (obj)	صُدُوْرِهِمْ	
433	The truth	اَلصِّدْق	★
434	Truthful (people) (obj)	صٰدِقِيْن	★
435	That which confirms, believes	مُصَدِّقًا	★
436	The path, the way, the road	اَلصِّرَاط	★

437	Virtuous, good, Salih (prophet)	صَالِحًا
438	The virtuous & good people	اَلصّٰلِحِيْنَ
439	The virtuous and good women, virtuous and good deeds	اَلصّٰلِحٰتُ
440	The Islamic worship (Ṡalat); The prayer	اَلصَّلٰوةُ
441	Calamity, trouble	مُصِيْبَةٌ
442	The horn that will be blown on the day of judgement	اَلصُّوْرُ
443	The terrible sound, outcry, shout	اَلصَّيْحَةُ
444	The dwelling, returning place	اَلْمَصِيْرُ
445	To point out a model, to strike on (a parable), to give example	ضَرَبَ
446	Loss, pain, calamity	ضُرٌّ

447	One who lost the (straight) path, wasted	ضَلَّ	★
448	Those who lost (straight) path, wasted	ضَلُّوْا	★
449	He misguides or will misguide	يُضِلُّ	★
450	Who is astrayed	يُّضْلِلِ	★
451	Error, straying from the right path or from the truth	ضَلٰلٌ	★
452	Food	طَعَام	
453	Name of mountain where Moses saw a fire, the Toor	اَلطُّوْرِ	
454	Obey (imperative) (pl)	اَطِيْعُوا	
455	Obey me (imp, pl)	اَطِيْعُوْنِ	
456	They have competence, ability, capability, faculty	يَسْتَطِيْعُوْنَ	
457	Party, group, people, denomination, minority	طَآئِفَةٌ	
458	Good and chaste	طَيِّبٰتٌ	
459	The bird	اَلطَّيْرُ	

460	The clay	اَلطِّيْن
461	They oppressed, they did wrong, injustice, ill-treated	ظَلَمُوْا
462	They oppress or will oppress, they do wrongs, injustice, ill-treat	يَظْلِمُوْنَ
463	They are oppressed or will be oppressed, mistreat	يُظْلَمُوْنَ
464	Oppressors or tyrants (subj)	ظٰلِمُوْن
465	Oppressors or tyrants (obj)	ظٰلِمِيْن
466	Who is more oppressive, who is more tyrant, darker, gloomier	اَظْلَمُ
467	Darknesses	ظُلُمٰت
468	The guess, thought, assumption, presumptions, the supposition	اَلظَّنّ
469	I worship or will worship	اَعْبُدُ *
470	You worship (pl) or will worship	تَعْبُدُوْنَ *
471	They worship or will worship	يَعْبُدُوْنَ *

472	You worship (pl) (imperative)	* اُعْبُدُوا
473	The servant, the slave, the worshipper	اَلْعَبْد
474	The servants, slaves, the people, mankind	اَلْعِبَاد
475	Our servants, our slaves	عِبَادِنَآ
476	His servants, his slaves	عِبَادِهٖ
477	My servants, my slaves	عِبَادِىْ
478	We have kept prepared, ready	اَعْتَدْنَا
479	He prepared, made ready, set-up	اَعَدَّ
480	Justice, fairness, honesty	* عَدْل
481	Garden of Eden, everlasting garden	عَدْن
482	Enemy	عَدُو
483	Enemy (obj)	عَدُوا
484	The punishment, the agony, the torture, the chastisement	* اَلْعَذَاب

485	Punishmet, agony (obj)	عَذَابًا ✦
486	The tribal Arabs, the Bedouin Arabs	اَلْاَعْرَاب
487	The throne (Al - 'Arsh)	اَلْعَرْش
488	Refuse, turn aside (imp, sing)	اَعْرِضْ
489	Those who refused	مُعْرِضُوْن
490	The recognised (practices), established (customs), universally accepted	اَلْمَعْرُوْف ✦
491	The dignity, respect, glory	اَلْعِزَّة
492	The mighty, the one who dominates	اَلْعَزِيْز
493	Perhaps, may be	عَسٰى
494	Great	عَظِيْم
495	Being great (obj)	عَظِيْمًا
496	The agony, the pain, the punishment, the penalty	اَلْعِقَاب
497	Result, end, the outcome, the consequence, the effect	عَاقِبَة *

498	You understand or will understand, comprehend, reason	تَعْقِلُوْنَ
499	They understand or will understand	يَعْقِلُوْنَ
500	He knew	عَلِمَ
501	I know or will know	اَعْلَمُ
502	You know or will know	تَعْلَمُ
503	You know (pl)	تَعْلَمُوْنَ
504	We know or will know	نَعْلَمُ
505	He knows or will know	يَعْلَمُ
506	They know or will know	يَعْلَمُوْنَ
507	Know, you (pl) be aware (imp)	اِعْلَمُوْآ
508	Knower, learned, acquainted, familiar (person)	عٰلِم
509	Known, appointed, fixed, determined, certainly, sure	مَعْلُوْم
510	I know or will know	اَعْلَمُ

511	All knowing, well acquainted, ever knowing	عَلِيمٌ
512	All knowing, well acquainted (obj)	عَلِيمًا
513	The knowledgeable, the omniscent	اَلْعَلِيمُ
514	Knowledge (obj)	عِلْمًا
515	The worlds, the universe	اَلْعٰلَمِينَ
516	Exalted, sublimed	تَعٰلٰى
517	He did, he practiced, he worked	عَمِلَ
518	They did, they practiced, they worked	عَمِلُوا
519	You do or will do (pl)	تَعْمَلُونَ
520	He does or will do	يَعْمَلُ
521	They do or will do	يَعْمَلُونَ
522	Their deeds (obj)	اَعْمَالَهُمْ
523	The blind	اَلْاَعْمٰى
524	Near, at, by, with	عِنْدَ

525	To us, with us, near us		عِنْدَنَا
526	To him, he has		عِنْدَهٗ
527	To them, with them, near them, they have		عِنْدَهُمْ
528	Promise, agreement		عَهْد
529	People of Ad followers of Prophet Hud		عَاد
530	Became angry, rage, fury, anger (verb, noun)		غَضَبَ
531	He pardons or will pardon	★	يَغْفِرُ
532	(Please) pardon or (please) forgive (imp)	★	اِغْفِرْ
533	Forgiving	★	غَفُوْر
534	Forgiving (obj)	★	غَفُوْرًا
535	Forgiveness, pardon	★	مَغْفِرَة
536	Saved		اَغْنٰى
537	Saves or will save, makes him wealthy		يُغْنِيْ
538	Unconcerned, rich, wealthy		غَنِيّ

539	The hidden, the unseen	★ اَلْغَيْب
540	Others, except, etc, other than, unlike	غَيْر
541	Except him or it, without him or it	غَيْرَه
542	The discord, the disorder, the test;, the dissension, the temptation	★ اَلفِتْنَة
543	Shameful deeds, abomination, adultery, fornication	فَاحِشَة
544	Pharaoh	فِرْعَوْن
545	A group (subj)	فَرِيْق
546	A group (obj)	فَرِيْقًا
547	Blamed, lied, falsified	اِفْتَرٰى
548	They blame or will blame, lie, falsify	يَفْتَرُوْنَ
549	Those who spread evil, transgressors (obj)	مُفْسِدِيْن
550	The reprobates, the great sinners, offenders	* اَلْفٰسِقُوْن

551	Reprobates, great sinners (obj)	* ٱلْفَٰسِقِينَ
552	The grace, the favor, the kindness	ٱلْفَضْلَ
553	Gracefully	فَضْلًا
554	His grace (obj)	فَضْلِهِۦ
555	He does or will do, performs	يَفْعَلُ
556	They do or will do	يَفْعَلُونَ
557	They comprehend or will comprehend, understand	يَفْقَهُونَ
558	They think deeply or will think deeply, ponder, contemplate	يَتَفَكَّرُونَ
559	Fruit(s)	فَاكِهَةً
560	You (pl) will prosper, succeed	★ تُفْلِحُونَ
561	the prosperous, the successful	★ ٱلْمُفْلِحُونَ
562	The boat, the vessel, the ship	ٱلْفُلْكُ

563	The success, the victory, the achievement, the accomplishment	اَلْفَوْزُ
564	On, upon, on top of, over, beyond	فَوْقَ
565	On them, upon them	فَوْقَهُمْ
566	Their mouths (obj)	اَفْوَاهِهِمْ
567	Before, previously, formerly, earlier	قَبْلُ
568	Before you (sing)	قَبْلِكَ
569	Before you (pl)	قَبْلِكُمْ
570	Before him (indir obj)	قَبْلِهٖ
571	Before them (indir obj)	قَبْلِهِمْ
572	The battle, the righteous war, the struggle, the fight	اَلْقِتَالُ
573	Has power over anything or will have	يَقْدِرُ
574	One who has power over any thing, ever powerful, the omnipotent	قَدِيْرٌ

575	(fem) forwarded, committed	قَدَّمَتْ
576	Al Quran (the Holy Book of Islam)	★ اَلْقُرْاٰن
577	Near, nearby, close at hand, in the neighborhood or vicinity	قَرِيْب
578	the close relatives, the kinship	اَلْقُرْبٰى
579	Very close, closer, nearer	اَقْرَبُ
580	The people, the previous centuries	اَلْقُرُوْن
581	The village, country (as opposed to a town)	اَلْقَرْيَة
582	The villages	اَلْقُرٰى
583	The division based on justice, fairness	اَلْقِسْط
584	Decided	قَضٰى
585	Was decided	قُضِىَ
586	Hearts, cores, minds, souls, spirits	قُلُوْب

587	Your hearts (pl)	قُلُوبُكُمْ
588	Their hearts (obj)	قُلُوبِهِمْ
589	Less in quantity, little	قَلِيل
590	Less in quantity, a little, seldom, rarely	قَلِيلًا
591	The moon	اَلْقَمَرُ
592	He said or told	قَالَ
593	She said or told	قَالَتْ
594	They said or told	قَالُوٓا
595	We said or told	قُلْنَا
596	You say (tell) or will say (tell) (sing)	تَقُوْلُ
597	You (pl) tell (cond, imp)	تَقُوْلُوا
598	You say (tell) or will say (tell)	تَقُوْلُوْنَ
599	We say (tell) or will say (tell)	نَقُوْلُ
600	He says (tells) or will say (tell)	يَقُوْلُ

601	He will certainly say (tell)	لَيَقُوْلُنَّ
602	They say (tell) or will (tell)	يَقُوْلُوْا
603	They say (tell) or will say (tell)	يَقُوْلُوْنَ
604	Say (you, sing) (imperative)	قُلْ
605	You (pl) tell (imperative)	قُوْلُوْا
606	Was told, was said	قِيْلَ
607	The saying, the statement	اَلْقَوْل
608	Saying	قَوْلًا
609	Their saying (indir. obj)	قَوْلِهِمْ
610	You stand or will stand, it stands	تَقُوْمُ
611	They established	اَقَامُوْا
612	You (pl) establish (imperative)	اَقِيْمُوْا
613	The staight, straight forwardness, the honest, the righteous	اَلْمُسْتَقِيْمُ ★

614	The appointed hour, the day of judgement, the day of resurrection	اَلْقِيٰمَةُ *
615	The people, the nation, fellow tribesmen	اَلْقَوْمُ
616	O my people!	يٰقَوْمِ
617	People	قَوْمًا
618	Your (sing) people, your ummah, your community, your followers	قَوْمُكَ
619	His people, his ummah	قَوْمُهٗ
620	Power, strength	قُوَّةٌ
621	Powerful, mighty, strong	قَوِيٌّ
622	They behaved proudly, arrogantly	اِسْتَكْبَرُوْا
623	Great	كَبِيْرٌ
624	Greatly	كَبِيْرًا
625	Greater	اَكْبَرُ
626	Was written, was enjoined	كُتِبَ ★

627	The Book, (the holy) book	اَلْكِتٰبُ	★
628	(Holy) book (obj)	كِتٰباً	★
629	More, much, many, plenty, numerous, abundant	كَثِيْرٌ	
630	More, much, many, plenty, (dir. obj)	كَثِيْرًا	
631	In plenty, abundance (fem)	كَثِيْرَ	
632	More often, more frequently	اَكْثَرَ	
633	Most of them	اَكْثَرُهُمْ	
634	Rejected, disbelieved, lied	كَذَّبَ	
635	(fem) rejected, disbelieved, lied	كَذَّبَتْ	
636	They rejected, disbelieved	كَذَّبُوْا	
637	You (both) reject (deny) or will reject (deny)	تُكَذِّبٰنِ	
638	The lie	اَلْكَذِبَ	
639	Lying	كَذِبًا	
640	Liars (subj)	كٰذِبُوْنَ	

641	Liars (obj)	كٰذِبِيْنَ
642	The liars (obj)	اَلْمُكَذِّبِيْنَ
643	Honourable, pleasant, generous, hospitable, kind, distinguished	كَرِيْمٌ
644	(It, she) earned, gained, acquired, attained	كَسَبَتْ
645	They earned, gained	كَسَبُوْا
646	They earn or will earn	يَكْسِبُوْنَ
647	(He) denied, hid (the truth), covered, disbelieved, cursed, sweared	كَفَرَ *
648	They denied, disbelieved, cursed	كَفَرُوْا *
649	You deny or will deny, disbelieve	تَكْفُرُوْنَ *
650	He denies or will deny, disbelieve	يَكْفُرُ *
651	They deny or will deny	يَكْفُرُوْنَ *
652	The denial (kufr), the disbelief	اَلْكُفْرُ *

653	Those who deny, those who cover (truth) (Kafirun, subj)	اَلْكٰفِرُوْنَ
654	Those who deny (truth, obj)	اَلْكٰفِرِيْنَ
655	Those who deny (truth)	اَلْكُفَّارُ
656	Is enough, to be enough, sufficient	كَفٰى
657	Everything, all, totality, entirety, everyone, each one	كُلُّ
658	Everything, all	كُلًّا
659	Whenever, at any time	كُلَّمَا
660	Never, not at all, on the contrary	كَلَّا
661	Saying, sentence, address speech, (kalima) remark	كَلِمَةٌ
662	He is, he was	كَانَ
663	They are, they were	كَانَتْ
664	They are, they were	كَانُوْا
665	You were (sing)	كُنْتَ
666	I was	كُنْتُ

667	You (pl) were	كُنْتُمْ
668	We were	كُنَّا
669	I become or I will become, I will be	أَكُونُ
670	Be or you be (imp, sing)	تَكُنْ
671	Be or become (imp, sing)	تَكُونُ
672	Be or you be (imp, sing)	تَكُونَنَّ
673	Be or you be (imp, pl)	تَكُونُوا
674	Be or he becomes or will become	يَكُنْ
675	Be or he becomes or will become	يَكُونُ
676	Be, they become or they will become	يَكُونُوا
677	Be (imp, sing)	كُنْ
678	Be (pl), become (imp)	كُونُوا
679	House, place, exchange, site, location, seat, position	مَكَان
680	How	كَيْفَ

681	The measure, the dry measure for grain	الْكَيْلَ
682	Intellectuals, those who have reasoning, and understanding, those who have minds and hearts and think rightly	ٱلْأَلْبَاب
683	So that you	لَعَلَّكُمْ
684	So that they, perhaps they may, maybe they	لَعَلَّهُمْ
685	Curse, damn	لَعْنَةَ
686	Put, throw, disregarded	أَلْقَى
687	Meeting, get together, reunion, in exchange for, in return for	لِقَآء
688	No, not, not to be, nothing else	لَيْسَ
689	The night, nightmare	ٱلَّيْل
690	Property, goods, pleasure, enjoyment, gratification, necessities of life	مَتَاع
691	Goods, property	مَتَاعًا

692	Like, similar, of the same kind	مِثْل
693	Like him, like it, similar to him (it)	مِثْلُهُ
694	Parable, example, proverb	مَثَل
695	example, for example, for instance	مَثَلاً
696	The examples, the metaphors, the parables	اَلْأَمْثَال
697	The city, the town	اَلْمَدِيْنَه
698	Name of city Mediyana	مَدْيَن
699	Woman, wife	اِمْرَاَة
700	(First or next) time, once	مَرَّة
701	Disease, sickness	مَرَض
702	The Messiah (Jesus)	اَلْمَسِيْح
703	With, along with	مَعَ
704	With you (sing)	مَعَكَ
705	With you (pl)	مَعَكُمْ

706	With him	مَعَهُ
707	With them	مَعَهُمْ
708	With me	مَعِيَ
709	The elite, the elders, the congregation, the audience	اَلْمَلَاُ
710	What their hands posessed, she (it, they fem) posessed, acquired	مَلَكَتْ
711	They possess power	يَمْلِكُوْنَ
712	Kingdom, power, reign, rule, sovereignty	مُلْك
713	The king, the monarch	اَلْمَلِك
714	Angel	مَلَك *
715	The angels	اَلْمَلٰٓئِكَةُ *
716	Creed, religion, religious community, denomination	مِلَّةٌ
717	The death	اَلْمَوْت
718	Her death, its death	مَوْتِهَا

719	The deceased ones, the dead ones	اَلْمَوْتٰى
720	The dead (body, person)	اَلْمَيِّت
721	The wealth, the money, the property, the possession	اَلْمَال
722	The wealths, the properties, the possessions	اَلْاَمْوَال
723	Your wealths (pl)	اَمْوَالُكُمْ
724	Their wealth	اَمْوَالُهُمْ
725	Water	مَآء
726	Incident, news, story, information	نَبَاء
727	Incidents, news, stories, announcements	اَنْبَآء
728	The prophet, the apostle	اَلنَّبِي
729	The prophets, the apostles	اَلنَّبِيّٖن
730	The Bible, holy book given to Jesus	اَلْاِنْجِيْل
731	Date tree, date palm	اَلنَّخْل

732	(He) called	نَادٰى
733	You warn or will warn	★ تُنْذِرُ
734	Warner	★ نَذِيْرٌ
735	Warner (obj)	★ نَذِيْرًا
736	He revealed, he sent	نَزَّلَ
737	We revealed, we sent	نَزَّلْنَا
738	He reveals or will reveal, he sends or will send	يُنَزِّلُ
739	He revealed, he sent	اَنْزَلَ
740	We revealed, we sent	اَنْزَلْنَا
741	We revealed it, we sent it	اَنْزَلْنٰهُ
742	That which was revealed or sent	اُنْزِلَ
743	Which is revealed slowly	تَنْزِيْلُ
744	The women, the wives	اَلنِّسَآءُ
745	They will be helped, assisted	يُنْصَرُوْنَ

746	The help, the aid, the assistance	اَلنَّصْر
747	Helpful, helper, ever helpful, supporter. protector (subj)	نَصِيْرٌ
748	Helpful, helper, ever helpful, protector, supporter (obj)	نَصِيْرًا
749	The Christains, the helpers	اَلنَّصٰرٰى
750	Sperm, drop	نُطْفَة
751	They see or will see, they wait or will wait, they perceive	يَنْظُرُوْنَ
752	Look, wait (imp, sing)	اُنْظُرْ
753	Bounty, favour, grace, blessing, benefaction	نِعْمَة
754	The delightful, happiness, felicity	اَلنَّعِيْم
755	The cattle, livestock	اَلْاَنْعَام
756	Wonderful, truly an excellent, what a good. . .	نِعْمَ
757	Individual, self, soul, psyche, spirit, mind, desire	نَفْس ★

758	Individual, self (obj)	★ نَفْساً
759	Yourself (indir. obj)	★ نَفْسِكَ
760	His soul, himself (indir. obj)	★ نَفْسِهِ
761	My soul, myself	★ نَفْسِي
762	Your souls, your lives, your selves	★ أَنْفُسَكُمْ
763	Their lives, themselves (indir obj)	★ أَنْفُسِهِمْ
764	They spent	أَنْفَقُوا
765	They spend or will spend	يُنْفِقُونَ
766	The hypocrites	★ اَلْمُنٰفِقِيْنَ
767	The evil, bad thing, abominable, objechionable, the forbidden	★ اَلْمُنْكَرَ
768	The rivers, the streams	اَلْاَنْهٰرِ
769	The daybreak, the daytime	اَلنَّهَارِ
770	The fire, the hell	★ اَلنَّارِ

771	Fire, fiery, burning, blazing, red-hot	★ نَارًا
772	The light, the brightness	اَلنُّوْر
773	The people, mankind, human being	اَلنَّاس
774	He guided, he lead to the right way	★ هَدٰى
775	He guides or he will guide, confer, bestow,	★ يَهْدِيْ
776	They guide or will guide, they are guided or will be guided	★ يَهْتَدُوْنَ
777	Guidance, right guidance true religion	★ هُدًى
778	(Harun) name of the brother of the Prophet Moses	هٰرُوْن
779	They mock at or will mock at, laugh, make fun	يَسْتَهْزِءُوْنَ
780	Mockery, ridicule	هُزُوًا
781	We destroyed	اَهْلَكْنَا
782	Jews, those who were guided	هَادُوْا

783	Desgraceful, dispised	مُهِيْن	
784	Their desires, whims, pleasures, likings, heretic tendencies	اَهْوَآءَهُمْ	
785	Covenant, treaty, agreement, contract, pact, alliance, charter	مِيْثَاق	
786	We found, found out	وَجَدْنَا	
787	You get or will get, find out	تَجِد	
788	They get or will get, find out	يَجِدُوْنَ	
789	Face, favour, sake, grace	وَجْه	
790	His face, his favour, his grace	وَجْهَهٗ	
791	Faces, prominent, leading (personalities, people)	وُجُوْه	
792	Their faces	وُجُوْهُهُمْ	
793	One, single, unique, without equal (masc)	وَاحِد	★
794	One (fem)	وَاحِدَة	★
795	We have revealed, we revealed	اَوْحَيْنَآ	★

796	(It was) revealed	أُوحِيَ	★
797	(He) reveals or will reveal	يُوحِي	★
798	Behind, in the rear of, at the back of, beside, in addition to	وَرَآء	
799	(He) promised, made a promise, pledge	وَعَدَ	
800	Which was promised to you	تُوعَدُونَ	
801	They are promised or will be promised	يُوعَدُونَ	
802	Promise	وَعْد	
803	You fulfill (imp, pl)	أَوْفُوا	
804	(They) had feared, safeguarded, protected	اِتَّقَوْا	*
805	You will fear (pl, neg; cond)	تَتَّقُوا	*
806	You will fear (pl)	تَتَّقُونَ	*
807	They fear or will fear	يَتَّقُونَ	*
808	You fear (imp, pl)	اِتَّقُوا	*

809	The piety, the godliness, devoutness, Taqwa	* ٱلتَّقْوَىٰ
810	The pious (people), the devout, the godly, righteous	* ٱلْمُتَّقِينَ
811	(He) has trust, trusts	يَتَوَكَّلْ
812	Advocate, protector, attorney, authorized representative	وَكِيلٌ
813	Advocate, protector, entrusted	وَكِيلًا
814	Son, child, boy, young one, descendant, offspring	وَلَدٌ
815	Progeny, son, daughter (dir obj)	وَلَدًا
816	Your (pl) sons, children	أَوْلَادُكُمْ
817	(He) turned back, turned away, seized power	★ تَوَلَّىٰ
818	(They) turned back	★ تَوَلَّوْا

819	Friend, leader (subj)	★ وَلِيّ
820	Close friend (dir obj)	★ وَلِيًّا
821	Friends, suporters, legal guardians, tutors, sponsors benefactors, protectors	★ اَوْلِيَآء
822	Nearest, woe, more entitled, more appropriate	★ اَوْلٰى
823	Woe, calamity, distress, affliction	وَيْل
824	The orphans, unique of their kind	اَلْيَتٰمٰى
825	In front of him, in his presence, in his power, his hands	يَدَيْهِ
826	Your (pl) hands (dir obj)	اَيْدِيَكُمْ
827	Their hands	اَيْدِيَهُمْ
828	They are certain, convinced sure or will be certain, convinced sure	يُوْقِنُوْنَ

829	The right hand, the right side, the lucky one	اَلْيَمِيْنِ
830	Your (pl) right hands, your oath, allegiance (indir obj)	اَيْمَانِكُمْ
831	Their right hands, their oaths, alligiance	اَيْمَانِهِمْ
832	The day (of judgement), age, era, time	اَلْيَوْمُ
833	Day (of judgement) sometimes, some day, one of these days	يَوْمًا
834	Days	اَيَّامُ
835	This day, today, at that time, then	يَوْمَئِذٍ

PART TWO

A List of 976 Words of the Quran whose frequency in the Quran is 5 to 9

with meanings in English

By knowing the words of the two lists one can understand 70.64 percent text of the Qur

1	Our father	أَبَانَا
2	My father	أَبَتِ
3	My father	أَبِيٓ
4	Their ancestors (obj)	آبَاءَهُمْ
5	Their ancestors (indir obj)	آبَاءِهِمْ
6	He disobeyed, refused	أَبَىٰ
7	Came, befell	أَتَىٰ
8	Came to you, reached you	أَتَىٰكَ
9	Came to them, reached them	أَتَىٰهُمْ
10	Cames to you, reaches you	يَأْتِكُمْ
11	They reach or will reach	يَأْتُوا
12	Comes to you or will come	يَأْتِيَكُم
13	(fem) they reach or will reach, to do, perform	يَأْتِينَ

14	Reaches him or will reach	يَأْتِيهِ
15	Come, bring (imp, sing)	اِئْتِ
16	Bring to us (imp, sing)	اِئْتِنَا
17	Come to me (imp) bring to me (imp, pl)	اِئْتُونِي
18	He brought to you, bestowed, he gave to you	اٰتٰكُمْ
19	They gave, performed	اٰتَوْا
20	You gave	اٰتَيْتُمْ
21	They give or will give	يُؤْتُونَ
22	He gives to him or will give	يُؤْتِيهِ
23	(Please) give to us	اٰتِنَا
24	Given to you, bestowed upon you	أُوتِيتُمْ
25	Their traces, tracks, marks, signs, (indir. obj)	اٰثَارِهِمْ
26	Sinner, criminal, wicked, evil	اٰثِيمٍ
27	My reward	أَجْرِيَ

28	Their (fem) rights, their (fem) rewards	أُجُوْرَهُنَّ
29	Their period (masc), term	أَجَلُهُمْ
30	Their period (fem), term	أَجَلَهُنَّ
31	One of you	أَحَدَكُمْ
32	One of them	أَحَدُهُمْ
33	One of the two	أَحَدِهِمَا
34	One (fem)	إِحْدَى
35	One of the two (fem)	إِحْدٰهُمَا
36	We siezed them, we took them	أَخَذْنٰهُمْ
37	Then he seized them	فَأَخَذَهُمْ
38	You (sing) take, catch hold (imp)	خُذْ

39	You take, you catch, you hold (imp, pl)	خُذُوْا
40	Is caught, will be caught	يُؤْخَذْ
41	You (pl) took, assumed	اِتَّخَذْتُمْ
42	They delay or will delay	يَسْتَاْخِرُوْنَ
43	Others or other people	اٰخَرُوْنَ
44	Others	اُخَرُ
45	His brother	اَخَاهُ
46	Their brother	اَخَاهُمْ
47	My brother	اَخِيْ
48	Your (pl) brothers	اِخْوَانُكُمْ
49	Their brothers	اِخْوَانِهِمْ
50	(He) permitted	اَذِنَ
51	Is permitted, will be permitted	يُؤْذَنُ
52	Ear, permissions	اُذُن

53	Their ears	أٰذَانِهِمْ
54	Pain, trouble, damage, harm, wrong, inconvenience	أَذًى
55	The thrones, couches, sofas	اَلْاَرَآئِك
56	Turn aside, hid, will turn aside	يُؤْفَكُوْنَ
57	Slander, lie, falsehood	اِفْك
58	You eat, or will eat	تَاْكُلُ
59	He eats or will eat	يَاْكُلُ
60	Mystic symbol (abbreviated letters, A.L.R.)	الٓرٰ
61	Thousand	اَلْف
62	Mystic symbol (abbreviated letters, A.L.M.)	الٓمٓ
63	Our gods (indir obj)	اٰلِهَتِنَا *
64	O, Allah!	اَللّٰهُمَّ
65	He decreed ordered, decreed	اَمَرَ ★

66	He decrees or will decree	يَأْمُرُ	★
67	He orders you (pl) or will order you	يَأْمُرُكُمْ	★
68	The order or will order	يَأْمُرُوْنَ	★
69	My Case	أَمْرِيْ	★
70	Mother, source, origin	أُم	
71	Your (pl) mothers	أُمَّهٰتِكُمْ	
72	Chiefs, leaders	أَئِمَّةً	
73	You accepted faith, you felt safe, you satisfied, you contended	آمِنْتُمْ	
74	(The community) accepted faith	اٰمَنَتْ	
75	You (pl) accept faith or will accept	تُؤْمِنُوْنَ	
76	Secured, peaceful	اٰمِنًا	
77	Secured, peaceful (pl)	اٰمِنِيْنَ	
78	Faith, belief, faithfully	إِيْمَانًا	

79	Your (pl) faith (indir obj)	* إِيمَانِكُمْ
80	Their faith	* إِيمَانُهُمْ
81	Believer, believing	* مُؤْمِنًا
82	Beleiver (fem)	* مُؤْمِنَةٌ
83	The two (fem)	اَلْاُنْثَيَيْنِ
84	Women, females	إِنٰثًا
85	People, human beings	أُنَاس
86	Your relatives, family members	اَهْلِكَ
87	Humbled, returnee	اَوَّاب
88	Abode, a place of return	مَاٰب
89	Interpretation	تَاْوِيْل
90	Its interpretation (dir obj)	تَاْوِيْلَهٗ
91	The earlier people, the ancestors, the fore fathers	اَلْاَوَّلُوْن
92	Now	اَلْئٰنَ

93 When أَيَّانَ

94 Where أَيْنَ

95 Who among them أَيُّهُمْ

96 To you alone, you beware (pl) إِيَّاكُمْ

97 To him alone إِيَّاهُ

98 With me alone, to me alone إِيَّايَ

99 Hardship, strength, fortitude بَأْس

100 He creates or will create, He starts or will start يَبْدَؤُا

101 Change, changing, exchanging تَبْدِيلا

102 Free, exempt, guiltless, innocent بَرِيٓي

103 Virtue, righteousness اَلْبِرَّ

104 We graced, blessed بٰرَكْنَا

105 Blessed, God bless تَبٰرَكَ

106	They give or will give glad tidings	يَسْتَبْشِرُونَ	★
107	Bearer of glad tidings	بَشِيرٌ	★
108	Bear of glad tidings	مُبَشِّراً	★
109	You see or will see, realize, understand, comprehend	تُبْصِرُونَ	
110	Insights, understanding, mental visions	بَصَآئِرُ	
111	The sight, vision, perceptions	اَلْبَصَرُ	
112	The liars, prattlers, windbags	اَلْمُبْطِلُونَ	★
113	Abdomen, internal parts, wombs, bellies	بُطُونٌ	
114	He sent	بَعَثَ	
115	We sent	بَعَثْنَا	
116	He raises or will raise, he sends or will send	يَبْعَثُ	
117	They will be raised, ressurected	يُبْعَثُونَ	
118	Will be raised (people)	مَبْعُوثُونَ	

119	Farther away, remoteness	بُعْدًا
120	Far, far away, remote, far reaching	بَعِيْدًا
121	After that (fem)	بَعْدِهَا
122	Some, portion, a few, a little of	بَعْضًا
123	The enmity, the hatred the hate	اَلْبَغْضَآءَ
124	The wish, desire, seek to attain	يَبْغُوْنَ
125	Long lasting, more durable	اَبْقٰى
126	Morning or tommorrow, tommorrow morning	بُكْرَةً
127	City, town, country, place, community	بَلَد
128	You ask for, aspire for, or will ask for	تَبْتَغُوْا
129	They ask for, aspire for, or will ask for	يَبْتَغُوْنَ
130	Proper, it's desirable, necessary, should be, ought to be	يَنْبَغِيْ

131	Rebellion, oppression, outrageous	بَغْيا	
132	The cities, the towns, the places	اَلْبِلَاد	
133	Earth, town, city, place	بَلْدَة	
134	He reaches, arrives or will reach	يَبْلُغ	★
135	Test, trial, tribulation, affliction, plague	بَلَآء	
136	Sons, children	اَبْنَآء	
137	Your (pl) sons, children	اَبْنَآءَكُمْ	
138	Their sons, children	اَبْنَآءَهُمْ	
139	O' my son	بُنَيَّ	
140	Houses	بُيُوْتا	
141	Your houses	بُيُوْتِكُمْ	
142	White, shining	بَيْضَآء	
143	Sale	بَيْع	

144	Between you (sing)	بَيْنَكَ
145	Between him	بَيْنَهُ
146	He followed you	اِتَّبَعَكَ
147	I follow or I will follow	أَتَّبِعُ ★
148	You follow (sing, imp)	تَتَّبِعُ ★
149	You (pl) follow (imp)	تَتَّبِعُوْا ★
150	We follow or we will follow	نَتَّبِعُ ★
151	He follows or he will follow	يَتَّبِعُ ★
152	You (sing) follow (imp)	اِتَّبِعُ ★
153	You (pl) follow (imp)	اِتَّبِعُوْا ★
154	Trade, business, commerce, merchandise	تِجَارَة
155	Under, beneath	تَحْتَ
156	Beneath them	تَحْتِهِمْ
157	Soil, dust, earth	تُرَاب

158	Soily, dusty	تُرَابًا	
159	We left	تَرَكْنَا	
160	You (sing) recite or will recite	تَتْلُوا	*
161	He recites or will recites	يَتْلُوا	*
162	They recite or will recite	يَتْلُونَ	*
163	You (sing) recite (imp)	اُتْلُ	*
164	Is recited or wil be recited	يُتْلٰى	*
165	He accomplishes or will accomplish	يُتِمُّ	
166	You (pl) repent (imp)	تُوبُوٓا	★
167	Repentance	تَوْبَة	★
168	Repentant, all repentant	تَوَّاب	★
169	Weight	مِثْقَال	
170	Three	ثَلٰث	
171	Reward	ثَوَاب	*
172	Abode, place	مَثْوًى	

173	All powerful	جَبَّار
174	Mountain	جَبَل
175	(They are) knelt down	جٰثِمِيْن
176	They refuse or will refuse, negate, denied	يَجْحَدُوْنَ
177	New, recent, modern, unprecedent	جَدِيْد
178	He quarrels or will quarrel, agrues, disputes	يُجَادِل
179	They quarrel or will quarrel, argue	يُجَادِلُوْنَ
180	Accountable, sin, doubtful, certainly, surely	لا جَرَم
181	He rewards them or will reward them	★ يَجْزِيَهُمْ
182	You (pl) are rewarded or will be rewarded	★ تُجْزَوْنَ
183	They are rewarded or will be rewarded	يُجْزَوْنَ
184	Their reward	★ جَزَآؤُهُمْ
185	He made you (pl)	جَعَلَكُمْ

186	We made her or it	جَعَلْنٰهَا
187	He made him or it	جَعَلَهٗ
188	You make or you will make	تَجْعَلُ
189	You (pl) make or will make	تَجْعَلُوْا
190	He makes (him or it) or will make	يَجْعَلُهٗ
191	They make or will make	يَجْعَلُوْنَ
192	Side, towards, partial view	جَانِب
193	Army, soldiers	جُنْد
194	Armies, soldiers	جُنُوْد
195	His armies, soldiers (indir. obj)	جُنُوْدِهٖ
196	Jinn, demon	جَآن
197	Endeavour, struggle, striving	جَهْد
198	Openness, clear loud voice	جَهْر
199	The ignorants, the illiterates	اَلْجٰهِلِيْن

200	They reply, accept or will reply	يَسْتَجِيبُوا
201	She (or that) came to you	جَآءَتْكُمْ
202	(It or He) came to us	جَآءَنَا
203	(It or He) came to him	جَآءَهُ
204	They came	جَآءُو
205	They came to you (sing)	جَآءُوكَ
206	You (sing) came	جِئْتَ
207	I came, brought to you (pl)	جِئْتُكُمْ
208	You (sing) came to us, brought	جِئْتَنَا
209	We came	جِئْنَا
210	You love or will love, you like or will like	تُحِبُّونَ
211	They like or will like	يُحِبُّونَ
212	Seed, grain, kernel	حَبَّةٌ

213	Became waste, wasted, lost	حَبِطَتْ
214	Rope, cable	حَبْلٌ
215	Veil, curtain, barrier, cover, partition	حِجَاب
216	The pilgrimage, (Al - Haj)	* اَلْحَج
217	Talk, speech, narative, fabulous story	★ حَدِيْثًا
218	Sayings	★ اَحَادِيْث
219	Iron, metal	حَدِيْد
220	Freedom, liberty	تَحْرِيْر
221	The inflamable, the scorched	اَلْحَرِيْق
222	We prohibited, we have forbidden	* حَرَّمْنَا
223	Party, group, troupe, band	حِـزْب
224	You worry or will worry	* تَحْزَنَ
225	That worries you	* يَحْزُنْكَ

226	Is enough	حَسِبَ	
227	You surely doubt or will doubt	تَحْسَبَنَّ	
228	He doubts or will doubt	يَحْسَب	
229	They doubt or will doubt	يَحْسَبُونَ	
230	Their account	حِسَابِهِمْ	★
231	Desire, wish, grief, sorrow, pain, distress, affliction, sigh	حَسْرَة	
232	He did well, perfected	أَحْسَنَ	★
233	They did well	أَحْسَنُوا	★
234	Good, handsome	حُسْن	★
235	Good, in a friendly manner	حُسْنا	★
236	The benefaction, the excellence	اَلْإِحْسَان	★
237	Benefaction, while performing good deeds, charity	إِحْسَانا	★
238	He will gather them	يَحْشُرُهُمْ	★
239	You are gathered or will be gathered	تُحْشَرُونَ	★

240	Chaste (women), protected	مُحْصَنٰت
241	(He) arrived	حَضَرَ
242	Those who will be called	مُحْضَرُوْن
243	Protectors (subj), care takers	حٰفِظُوْن
244	Protectors (obj), care takers	حٰفِظِيْن
245	Protector	حَفِيْظ
246	Came true	حَقَّتْ ★
247	You (sing) decide (imp)	اُحْكُمْ
248	Decree, decision	حُكْمًا
249	The judges, the rulers, the governors	اَلْحٰكِمِيْن
250	He permits or will permit, falls , will fall	يَحِل
251	Is permitted, lawful	حَلٰلًا
252	Lawfully, rightly	اُحِل
253	Mystic symbol (H . M) (abbreviated letters)	حٰمٓ

254	You put weight or will put, you carry weight or will carry	تَحْمِلُ
255	He encircled	اَحَاطَ
256	One who encircles, surrounding, comprehensive	مُحِيْط
257	Around him or it	حَوْلَهٗ
258	Befell, surrounded	حَاقَ
259	(He) gave life	اَحْيَا
260	He gives life to you (pl) or will give	يُحْيِيْكُمْ
261	He who is alive, alive	حَيًّا
262	Those who are alive, alive (pl)	اَحْيَاءٌ
263	Name of Prophet (Yahaya)	يَحْيٰى
264	The bad, the wicked, the malicious	اَلْخَبِيْثُ

265	They left, went out	خَرَجُوْا
266	She/it comes out or will come out	تَخْرُجُ
267	They come out or will come out	يَخْرُجُوْا
268	You (sing) come out (imp)	أُخْرُجْ
269	We brought out	أَخْرَجْنَا
270	We bring you out or will bring you out	نُخْرِجُ
271	He brings you out or will bring you out	يُخْرِجُكُم
272	Exit, outlet, escape	خُرُوْجٌ
273	He fell	خَرَّ
274	Treasures	خَزَآئِن
275	He suffered loss	خَسِرَ
276	They suffered loss	خَسِرُوْا
277	Fearful, obedient, humble, submissive	خٰشِعِيْن
278	With fear, fearfully	خَاشِعَةً

279	He fears or will fear	يَخْشٰى
280	They fear or will fear	يَخْشَوْنَ
281	Fear, anxiety	خَشْيَةً
282	Paths, footsteps	خُطُوٰت
283	Will be lessened, will be reduced	يُخَفَّفُ
284	The permanence, the ever-lasting	اَلْخُلْدُ
285	Pure, clear, unadulterated	خَالِصَةً
286	Sincere (pl)	مُخْلِصِيْنَ
287	The sincere (ones)	اَلْمُخْلَصِيْنَ
288	He breaches promise or will breach	يُخْلِفُ
289	You create differences or will create	تَخْتَلِفُوْنَ
290	Behind	خِلَافَ
291	Difference, change	اِخْتِلَاف
292	(You) created (sing)	خَلَقْتَ
293	(We) created you (pl)	خَلَقْنٰكُمْ

294 Was created خُلِقَ

295 Creature, creation خَلْقًا

296 Creator خَالِق

297 They retired, to be alone خَلَوْا

298 (He) feared خَافَ

299 You (pl) feared خِفْتُمْ

300 You (sing) fear (imp) تَخَفْ

301 (He) fears or will fear يَخَفْ

302 Bent, devastated خَاوِيَة

303 Those who turn and flee مُدْبِرِيْن

304 Backs, turning backs اَدْبَار

305 Their backs, turning their backs اَدْبَارَهُمْ

306 He entered, came in دَخَلَ

307 You (pl) enter or will enter تَدْخُلُوا

308	They enter or will enter	يَدْخُلُوْنَ
309	He makes to enter, he gets entered or will get entered	يُدْخِلُ
310	He lets him enter or will let him enter	يُدْخِلُهُ
311	He lets them enter or will let them enter	يُدْخِلُهُمْ
312	He called, he prayed, he summoned, he sent for	دَعَا
313	They called, they prayed	دَعَوْا
314	You (pl) call or will call	تَدْعُوْا
315	You (pl) call them or will call them	تَدْعُوْهُمْ
316	He calls or will call	يَدْعُ
317	They invite or will invite	يَدْعُوْآ
318	Blood	دَم
319	Loan, debt, liability, obligation, financial claim	دَيْن

320	Particle, atom		ذَرَّةٍ
321	His descendants, offspring		ذُرِّيَّتِهِ
322	They remember or will remember	★	يَذْكُرُونَ
323	Was remembered, mentioned, was recited	★	ذُكِرَ
324	Remember (imp, sing) remind	★	ذَكِّرْ
325	They were reminded	★	ذُكِّرُوا
326	He gives advice or will give, remembers	★	يَتَذَكَّرُ
327	They give advice or will give, remember	★	يَتَذَكَّرُونَ
328	He learns lesson or will learn lesson	★	يَذَّكَّرُ
329	They consider or will consider	★	يَذَّكَّرُونَ
330	My remembrance, my reminder	★	ذِكْرِي

331	Reminder, memento	★ تَذْكِرَة
332	One who learns a lesson	★ مُدَّكِر
333	Insult, humiliation, disgrace	ذِلَّة
334	Your (pl) sins	ذُنُوبَكُم
335	Our sins	ذُنُوبَنَا
336	He went, travelled	ذَهَبَ
337	Go (imp, sing)	إِذْهَبْ
338	The gold	اَلذَّهَب
339	Their heads (indir. obj)	رُءُوسِهِمْ
340	He saw him, he saw it	رَاٰهُ
341	I saw them	رَاَيْتُهُمْ
342	I see or I will see, envision	اَرٰى
343	We see or we sill see	نَرٰى
344	We see you (sing) or will see	نَرٰكَ

345	He sees or will see, he envisions	يَرَىٰ
346	They envision, see or will see	يَرَوْنَ
347	He shows you or will show	يُرِيكُمْ
348	Her God, lord (Rubb)	رَبُّهَا
349	You (pl) wait (imp)	تَرَبَّصُوا
350	Four	أَرْبَعَة
351	The usury, the interest (riba)	اَلرِّبٰوا
352	Chastisement, agony, calamity	رِجْز
353	Filthy, shameful, dirty	رِجْس
354	You (pl) go back (imp), return	اِرْجِعُوٓا
355	He will be returned	تُرْجَع
356	They will be returned, brought back	يُرْجَعُوْنَ
357	Their returning place	مَرْجِعُهُمْ
358	Person, man	رَجُلًا

359	People, on foot	رِجَالًا
360	Your (pl) feet	اَرْجُلَكُمْ
361	Their feet (indir. obj)	اَرْجُلِهِمْ
362	Acursed, outcast, damned	رَجِيْمٍ
363	They hope or will hope	يَرْجُوْا
364	You are blessed or will be blessed	تُرْحَمُوْنَ
365	Our blessing, mercy	رَحْمَتِنَا
366	The merciful (pl', obj)	اَلرّٰحِمِيْنَ
367	The wombs, kinship, relationship	اَلْاَرْحَامَ
368	Is returned or will be returned	يُرَدُّ
369	He gave you (pl) food, nourishment	رَزَقَكُمُ
370	We gave you (pl) food we have provided you with food	رَزَقْنٰكُمْ
371	He gives you (pl) food or will give, he provides you with food or will provide	يَرْزُقُكُمْ

372	Those who provide (food)	اَلرّٰزِقِيْن	
373	He sent	اَرْسَلَ	*
374	We send or will send	نُرْسِل	*
375	You send (imp, sing)	اَرْسِلْ	*
376	Messages	رِسٰلٰت	*
377	Those who were sent as Prophets or messengers	مُرْسَلُوْن	*
378	Mountains, unshakable mountains	رَوَاسِيَ	
379	Guidance, integrity of conduct	رَشَدًا	
380	(He) agreed, was pleased	رَضِيَ	
381	They agreed They were pleased	رَضُوْا	
382	He agreed or will agree, he rejoices or will rejoice	يَرْضٰى	
383	Pleasure, delight, consent, agreement, approval	رِضْوَان	
384	He raised	رَفَعَ	

385	We raised	رَفَعْنَا
386	Neck, slave, person	رَقَبَةٌ
387	They intended, they wanted	أَرَادُوا
388	We intended, we wanted	أَرَدْنَا
389	I intend or will intend	أُرِيدُ
390	You (pl) wish or will wish	تُرِيدُونَ
391	We wish or will wish	نُرِيدُ
392	Whoever wishes, intends, wants	يُرِدْ
393	Uncertain, suspicious	مُرِيبٌ
394	Old Testament, scriptures	الزُّبُرُ
395	Crops, vegetation, sowing, plantation	زَرْعٌ
396	You imagined, pretended, alleged, claimed	زَعَمْتُمْ
397	Name of Prophet (Zachariah)	زَكَرِيَّا

398	He purifies them or will purfiy	يُزَكِّيهِمْ *
399	Pair, husband, spouse, mate Two pairs, two mates, two spouses	زَوْج
400	Pairs (dir obj)	زَوْجَيْنِ
401	Your (pl) wives	أَزْوَاجُكُمْ
402	He increased them	زَادَهُمْ
403	He increases or will increase	يَزِيدُ
404	He increases for them or will increase	يَزِيدُهُمْ
405	He decorated, adorned	زَيَّنَ
406	We adorned, decorated	زَيَّنَّا
407	You (sing) ask (imp)	سَأَلْتَهُمْ
408	You ask (imp)	إِسْئَلْ
409	You will be asked	تُسْئَلُونَ
410	They inquire or will inquire	يَتَسَاءَلُونَ

411	Saturday	اَلسَّبْت	
412	(He) praises, glorifies	يُسَبِّحُ	*
413	They pray or will pray, praising, glorifying	يُسَبِّحُوْنَ	*
414	Glory be to you	سُبْحٰنَكَ	*
415	(She) overtook	سَبَقَتْ	
416	Ways, roads, pathway, method	سُبُلًا	
417	Six	سِتَّة	
418	They prostrated	سَجَدُوْا	
419	(You) prostrate (imp., pl)	اُسْجُدُوْا	
420	Mosques, places where Muslims pray and prostrate	مَسَاجِد	
421	The jail, the prison	اَلسِّجْن	
422	Clouds	سَحَاب	
423	The magicians, the witches, the wizards	اَلسَّحَرَة	

424	They concealed, they hid, they kept it secret	أَسَرُّوا
425	Secretly	سِرًّا
426	Couches, beds	سُرُر
427	They are hasty, they come in a hurry	يُسَارِعُوْنَ
428	March go (imp) (you sing)	أَسْرِ
429	Stories, tales, fables, legends	أَسَاطِيْرُ
430	The blazing fire, the hell	اَلسَّعِيْرُ
431	Blazing fire, blazing flame	سَعِيْرًا
432	He endeavoured, he moved quickly	سَعٰى
433	He runs or will run "attempts"	يَسْعٰى
434	Journey	سَفَر

435	The fools, the foolish, the stupid, the insolent fellows	اَلسُّفَهَاءُ	
436	Their abodes, their houses	مَسٰكِنِهِمْ	
437	Poor, beggar, miserable, humble	مِسْكِيْن	
438	He passed, it happened	سَلَفَ	
439	He accepted (Islam)	اَسْلَمَ	*
440	Greeting, peace, peacefully	سَلٰمًا	*
441	Islam (The religion of peace)	اَلْاِسْلَام	*
442	They heard, listened	سَمِعُوْا	
443	He hears or will hear	يَسْمَعُ	
444	You make them listen	تُسْمِعُ	
445	They listen or will listen they are listening	يَسْتَمِعُوْ	
446	Their hearing (indir. obj)	سَمْعِهِمْ	
447	His name	اِسْمُهٗ	

448	Year	سَنَة
449	(fem) Became evil, bad, wicked	سَاءَتْ
450	Evil, ill, misfortune, calamity	اَلسُّوْء
451	Evil, sin, sinfully	سُوْٓءًا
452	Your sins, your ill deeds	سَيِّاٰتِكُمْ
453	Their sins, their ill deeds	سَيِّاٰتِهِمْ
454	Surah (Chapter in the Quran)	سُوْرَة
455	Their signs, marks, expressions	سِيْمَاهُمْ
456	They travel or will travel, are travelling	يَسِيْرُوْا
457	You (pl) travel (imp)	سِيْرُوْا
458	The trees, bushes, shrubs	الشَّجَر
459	His full strength	اَشُدَّهٗ

460	You (pl) drink (imp)	اِشْرَبُوا	
461	Liquor, drink, (noun)	شَرَاب	
462	The east	اَلْمَشْرِق	
463	I associate or will, associate am associating	اُشْرِكُ	*
464	You (pl) associate or will associate, are associating	تُشْرِكُوْن	*
465	He associates or will associate, is associating	يُشْرِكُ	*
466	Their associates, partners	لِشُرَكَآءِہِمْ	
467	My associates, partners	شُرَكَآءِ یَ	
468	Those who associate others with Allah	اَلْمُشْرِكُوْن	*
469	They bought, they purchased	اِشْتَرَوا	
470	They buy, or will buy, transact, are buying	يَشْتَرُوْنَ	
471	Name of a Prophet (Shuaib)	شُعَيْبا	

472	Intercessor, advocate, mediator	شَفِيع	*
473	Quarrel, difference, trouble	شِقَاق	
474	They thank, will thank, are thanking	يَشْكُرُوْنَ	
475	You (pl) thank (imp)	أُشْكُرُوْا	
476	Those who are grateful, appreciating	اَلشّٰكِرِيْنَ	
477	Grateful, appreciating	شَكُوْر	
478	The north	اَلشِّمَال	
479	He witnessed, he bore witness	شَهِدَ	★
480	They witnessed, they bore witness	شَهِدُوْا	★
481	He bears witness or will bear, he sees or will see, is witness-ing, seeing	يَشْهَدُ	★
482	Witnesses, witnessing	شٰهِدِيْنَ	★

483	Months	اَشْهُر	
484	They desire or will desire, are desiring	يَشْتَهُوْنَ	
485	You desired, wanted, wished	شِئْتُمْ	
486	We intended	شِئْنَا	
487	You (sing) desire or will desire, are desiring	تَشَآءُ	
488	They desire or will desire desiring	يَشَآءُوْنَ	
489	He entered into morning, he became	اَصْبَحَ	
490	Those who entered into morning	مُصْبِحِيْنَ	
491	You (pl) patiently bear or will bear	تَصْبِرُوْا	★
492	You (pl) patiently bear or will bear	إِصْبِرُوْا	★
493	The patience, steadfastness	اَلصَّبْرُ	★

494	With patience, patiently	صَبْرًا	★
495	The commandments, the books	اَلصُّحُف	
496	They created hinderance, obstacle	صَدُّوْا	
497	They create hindrance or will create, creating hindrance	يَصُدُّوْنَ	
498	They accepted truth	صَدَقُوْا	★
499	He certified, testified	صَدَّقَ	★
500	The truthful (ones)	اَلصّٰدِقُوْن	★
501	Alm, charity	صَدَقَة	★
502	The alms, the charities	اَلصَّدَقٰت	★
503	One who certifies, attests	مُصَدِّق	★
504	Path, road, way	صِرَاط	★
505	We illustrated, displayed	صَرَّفْنَا	
506	The blast, the thunderbolt the bolt of lightning	اَلصّٰعِقَة	
507	Group, in a group	صَفًّا	
508	He amends	اَصْلَحَ	

509	They amended (themselves)	أَصْلَحُوْا	
510	Prophet Salih, virtuous (man or deed)	صَالِح	
511	Deaf	صُمّ	
512	Their prayer (salat)	صَلَاتِهِمْ	*
513	They make, are making	يَصْنَعُوْنَ	
514	He reached, hit	أَصَابَ	
515	Reached them, hit them	أَصَابَهُمْ	
516	Reached them, are hit	تُصِبْهُمْ	
517	He reaches or will reach hit, reaching, hitting	يُصِيْبُ	
518	The fasting	اَلصِّيَام	*
519	The prey, the game, (animal or bird), what is hunted	اَلصَّيْد	
520	We hit, on a parable, coined	ضَرَبْنَا	
521	He hits or will hit, he strikes (parable)(imp) or will strike	يَضْرِب	

522	You (sing) hit (imp) you strike (parable)(imp)	اِضْرِبْ
523	Harm, damage, injury	ضَرًّا
524	The adversity, the bad days	اَلضَّرَّآءِ
525	Those who were considered as weak, those who were made weak	اُسْتُضْعِفُوْا
526	He goes astray or will go, he misleads or will mislead, is misleading	يَضِلُّ
527	He mislead	اَضَلَّ
528	The misguided people (subj)	اَلضَّآلُّوْنَ
529	The misguided people (obj)	اَلضَّآلِّيْنَ
530	More or most misguided	اَضَلُّ
531	Error, in a state of err	ضَلٰلًا
532	The error, the err, the misguidance	اَلضَّلٰلَةَ
533	He wastes or will waste, wasting	يُضِيْعُ

534	Flooded, he rebelled, exceeded proper boundaries, became excessive	طَغَىٰ
535	Their rebellion, tyranny, oppression, terrorization	طُغْيَانِهِمْ
536	Defiance, the idol, the false god, the tyrant, the oppressor	اَلطَّاغُوتُ
537	He gets satisfied, or will get, getting satisfied	تَطْمَئِنَّ
538	Chaste, In a state of purity, clean	مُطَهَّرَةٌ
539	We obeyed	اَطَعْنَا
540	Do not obey (imp) (sing)	لَا تُطِعِ
541	If you (pl) obey	اِنْ تُطِيعُوا
542	Whoever obeys	مَنْ يُّطِعِ
543	You have competence, you have ability, capacity	اِسْتَطَعْتُمْ
544	The good, the pure	اَلطَّيِّبَ

545	Goodly, purely		طَيِّبًا
546	Goodly, purely (fem)		طَيِّبَةً
547	The shade, the shadow the shelter		الظِّلِّ
548	Oppression, tyranny, transgression	★	ظُلْمٌ
549	Wrongfully	★	ظُلْمًا
550	Oppressor, wrong-doer	★	ظَالِمٌ
551	Great Oppressor	★	ظَلَّامٌ
552	He doubted, assumed, presumed		ظَنَّ
553	You (pl) doubted, supposed		ظَنَنْتُمْ
554	They doubted		ظَنُّوٓا
555	They doubt or will doubt, are doubting		يَظُنُّوْنَ
556	It appeared, became visible, obvious		ظَهَرَ

557	Their backs, appearances	ظُهُورِهِمْ	
558	You (pl) worship or will worship, are worshipping	تَعْبُدُوٓا	*
559	We worship or will worship, are worshipping	نَعْبُدُ	*
560	He worships or will worship, is worshipping	يَعْبُدُ	*
561	You (pl) worship Him	اُعْبُدُوْهُ	*
562	Servant, slave	عَبْدًا	
563	Our servant	عَبْدِنَا	
564	His servant	عَبْدِهِ	
565	Your (sing) servants	عِبَادِكَ	
566	For the servants	لِلْعَبِيْدِ	
567	Worshippers (subj)	عٰبِدُوْنَ	*
568	Worshippers (obj)	عٰبِدِيْنَ	*
569	Lesson, moral, warning	عِبْرَةً	

570	Do not wander, don't do harm, don't cause mischief, don't act wickedly	لَا تَعْثَوْا
571	Those who make helpless, those who defeat, those who are weak, feeble, powerless	★ مُعْجِزِيْنَ
572	You make haste	تَسْتَعْجِلُوْنَ
573	Calf	اَلْعِجْلَ
574	Period, number, waiting period for a widowed or divorced woman	عِدَّة
575	They do justice, or will do, or are doing justice	* يَعْدِلُوْنَ
576	The transgressors, the assailants, the aggressors	اَلْمُعْتَدِيْنَ
577	Enemies	اَعْدَآء
578	The enmity, hostility, animosity	اَلْعَدَاوَة
579	The gross injustice, the aggres-sion	اَلْعُدْوَان
580	He punishes them or will punish, is punishing them	★ يُعَذِّبَهُمْ
581	My punishment	★ عَذَابِيْ

582	Arabic, Arabian, Literary Arabic	عَرَبِيًّا
583	He turned aside, shunned, avoided	أَعْرَضَ
584	Those who turn aside, those who shun away	مُعْرِضِيْنَ
585	Incidental (goods)	عَرَضَ
586	Knownly, goodly, properly	مَعْرُوفًا ★
587	Mighty, mightly	عَزِيْزًا
588	In the evening	بِالْعَشِيِّ
589	You (sing) stick, rod, cane	عَصَاكَ
590	They disobeyed	عَصَوْا
591	Your (sing) stick, rod, cane	عَصَيْتُ
592	Bones, in a stae of being bones, being in a form of bones	عِظَامًا
593	He forgave	عَفَا
594	End, result	عُقْبَى *

595	Clot of blood, leech, coagulated blood,	عَلَقَة
596	You (pl) knew	عَلِمْتُمْ
597	We knew	عَلِمْنَا
598	You know or will know, are knowing	تَعْلَمُوا
599	They know or will know	يَعْلَمُوٓا
600	Shortly they will know	سَيَعْلَمُوْنَ
601	His knowledge	عِلْمِهٖٓ
602	They declare, they proclaim	يُعْلِنُوْنَ
603	You (pl) come (imp)	تَعَالَوْا
604	The high, the great, the sublime, the most high, the supreme,	اَلْعَلِيّ
605	The highest, the greatest	اَلْاَعْلٰى
606	She worked, did, carried out,	عَمِلَتْ
607	We work or will work, are working	نَعْمَل

608	اِعْمَلُوْا	You (pl) work (imp)
609	عَمَلٌ	Action, work (subj)
610	عَمَلًا	Action, work (obj) workingly
611	عَمَلَهٗ	His work, his deed
612	اَعْمَالُكُمْ	Your (pl) works, your deeds
613	يَعْمَهُوْنَ	Blindly wander, going astray
614	اَعْنَاب	Grapes
615	عِنْدِكَ	From you (sing), with you (sing) you have, in your opinion
616	عِنْدِيْ	To me, with me, I have
617	عَهْدَهُمْ	Their promise
618	عِوَجًا	Crooked, deviation
619	يُعِيْدُهٗ	He brings him back or will bring him back, he is bringing him back
620	اَعُوْذُ	I seek refuge or will seek refuge

621	Eye, sauna, fountain head,	عَيْن
622	Eye, stream	عَيْنًا
623	Steams, spring,	عُيُوْن
624	Eyes,	أَعْيُن
625	Their eyes	أَعْيُنِهِمْ
626	Those who are left those who are gone, in the past	الْغٰبِرِيْن
627	The west, the sunset	اَلْمَغْرِب
628	Deception, in a state of misleading	غُرُوْرًا
629	We drowned	أَغْرَقْنَا
630	It covers or will cover, over covers, wraps up	يَغْشٰى
631	He got angry, mad, irritated	غَضِبَ
632	You ask for forgiveness (imp)	★ اَسْتَغْفِر

633	You (pl) ask for forgiveness (imp)	★ اَسْتَغْفِرُوا
634	One who is neglectful (indir obj)	بِغَافِلٍ
635	Those who are neglectful (subj)	غَافِلُونَ
636	Those who are neglectful (obj)	غَافِلِينَ
637	Neglect, negligence, inattention	غَفْلَةٌ
638	Those who are conquerors	غَالِبُونَ
639	Hard, severe	غَلِيظٌ
640	Slave, child, son	غُلَامٌ
641	Grief, affliction, sorrow, distress	غَمٌّ
642	Makes or will make unconcerned, saves or will save	تُغْنِيَ
643	Hearts	اَفْئِدَةٌ

644	Group, class, troop, band	فِئَةٌ	
645	We opened, turned on, introduced, began	فَتَحْنَا	
646	The victory, the success	اَلْفَتْحُ	
647	We tested, tempted	فَتَنَّا	★
648	The dawn, the opening, appcarance	اَلْفَجْرُ	
649	The evil or the shameful deeds	اَلْفَحْشَآءُ	★
650	They enjoyed, they rejoiced	فَرِحُوْا	
651	Duty, that which is enjoined, obligation	فَرِيْضَةٌ	
652	That which differentiates (between right & wrong)	اَلْفُرْقَانُ	
653	(He) spread evil or will spread evil	اِفْتَرَاهُ	
654	They trangress, or will transgress, transgressing	يُفْسِدُوْنَ	★
655	The mischief, the transgression	اَلْفَسَادُ	★

656	They defy or will defy	يَفْسُقُونَ *
657	We explain in detail or will explain	نُفَصِّلُ
658	The decision, the judgement	اَلْفَصْلُ
659	The silver	اَلْفِضَّةُ
660	He gave preference, he gave distinction	فَضَّلَ
661	Creator	فَاطِرُ
662	Worked, performed	فَعَلَ
663	They did it, they commited it.	فَعَلُوهُ
664	You (pl) do or will do	تَفْعَلُوا
665	Whatever you do or will do	مَا تَفْعَلُونَ
666	Those who do, those who commit	فٰعِلِيْنَ
667	Executed, fulfilled	مَفْعُولًا
668	The poor, the beggars	اَلْفُقَرَآءُ
669	Do not or will not succeed	لَا يُفْلِحُ ★
670	Upon you	فَوْقَكُمْ

671	The Graves	اَلْقُبُوْر	
672	(He) killed	قَتَلَ	
673	You (pl) kill or will kill	تَقْتُلُوْا	
674	You (pl) kill or will kill	تَقْتُلُوْنَ	
675	They kill or will kill	يَقْتُلُوْنَ	
676	You (pl) kill (imp)	اُقْتُلُوْآ	
677	Was killed	قُتِلَ	
678	Were killed (pl)	قُتِلُوْا	
679	They fight you or will fight	يُقَاتِلُوْكُمْ	
680	They fight or will fight	يُقَاتِلُوْنَ	
681	You (pl) fight (imp)	قَاتِلُوْا	
682	The murder, the killing	اَلْقَتْل	
683	He fixed, decreed, destined	قَدَّرَ	★
684	Mighty, competent, powerful	قَادِر	★

685 Those who are mighty, competent — قٰدِرُوْنَ

686 (One who is) mighty, Almighty — قَدِيْرًا

687 (He) balanced, measured. — قَدَرَ

688 You do not go near — لَا تَقْرَبُوْا

689 Near, nearby, vicinity — قَرِيْبًا

690 The Abode, the place, dwelling, habitation, resting place — اَلْقَرَارُ

691 Abode, place, set time — مُسْتَقَرٌّ

692 Loan, interest free loan — قَرْضًا

693 The calamity, the hour of the last judgement — اَلْقَارِعَةُ

694 Centuries, generations — قَرْنٌ

695 They sweared — اَقْسَمُوْا

696 (I) swear or will swear — اُقْسِمُ

697 (We) narrate or will narrate (stories) — نَقُصُّ

698 (He) decides or will decide — يَقْضِيْ

699	They turned around, about	اِنْقَلَبُوْا *
700	He turns or will turn	يَنْقَلِب *
701	Heart, middle, center, core	قَلْب *
702	His heart	قَلْبِهٖ *
703	Our hearts	قُلُوْبُنَا *
704	His shirt	قَمِيْصِهٖ
705	The most dominant, the subduer	اَلْقَهَّار
706	You (sing) said	قُلْتَ
707	I said	قُلْتُ
708	You (pl) said	قُلْتُمْ
709	I say or will say	اَقُلْ
710	I say or will say	اَقُوْل
711	He stands or will stand	يَقُوْمُ *
712	They establish or will establish	يُقِيْمُوْنَ *
713	You establish (imp, sing)	اَقِمْ *

714	Standing	قَآئِمًا	*
715	Standing (fem)	قَآئِمَةً	*
716	While standing	قِيٰمًا	*
717	Place, standing place	مَقَامٍ	*
718	One who establishes, ever-lasting	مُقِيْمٌ	*
719	Straight	مُسْتَقِيْمًا	★
720	Their people	قَوْمَهُمْ	
721	My people, nation, tribe	قَوْمِيْ	
722	Numerous, many	كَأَيِّنْ	
723	Grieved, offended, hated	كَبُرَ	
724	They feel proud or will feel proud	يَسْتَكْبِرُوْنَ	
725	The old age	اَلْكِبَرُ	
726	The great one (fem)	اَلْكُبْرٰى	

727	He wrote	كَتَبَ	★
728	We wrote, we prescribed, we fixed	كَتَبْنَا	★
729	They write or will write	يَكْتُبُوْنَ	★
730	His book, his account	كِتٰبَهٗ	★
731	You conceal or will conceal	تَكْتُمُوْنَ	
732	They conceal or will conceal	يَكْتُمُوْنَ	
733	They refused him, disbelieved	كَذَّبُوْهُ	
734	You refuse or will refuse, you deny or will deny	تُكَذِّبُوْنَ	
735	He refuses or will refuse	يُكَذِّبُ	
736	Liar	كَذَّاب	
737	Repetition	كَرَّةً	
738	He disliked	كَرِهَ	
739	Hateful, unwilling	كَرْهًا	
740	Those who dislike	كٰرِهُوْنَ	

741	We unveiled	كَشَفْنَا	
742	You (pl) dis believed, you were ungrateful	كَفَرْتُمْ	*
743	They reject, they disbelieve	يَكْفُرُوا	*
744	He will cover, forgive, he will hide	يُكَفِّرْ	*
745	Disbelieve, disbelieving	كُفْرًا	*
746	Their disbelief	كُفْرِهِمْ	*
747	Disbeliever (kafir)	كَافِرٌ	*
748	Ungratefulness	كَفُورٌ	*
749	Completely, altogether	كَآفَّةً	
750	All of it, all belong to (masc)	كُلِّهِ	
751	All of it, all belong to (fem)	كُلُّهَا	
752	Words	كَلِمٰتُ	
753	His words	كَلِمٰتِهِ	
754	Shortly	يَكَادُ	
755	I will be, I will become	أَكُنْ	

756	You (sing) are or will	تَكُ
757	We will be	نَكُونَ
758	Verily we shall be	لَنَكُونَنَّ
759	He is or will be	يَكُ
760	House, place	مَكَانا
761	So that not	لِكَيْلَا
762	Plot, deceit, compiracy	كَيْدُ
763	Plot, plotting	كَيْدًا
764	You (sing) stayed	لَبِثْتَ
765	I stayed	لَبِثْتُ
766	You stayed, remained	لَبِثْتُمْ
767	They stayed, remained	لَبِثُوا
768	Flesh, meat	لَحْمُ

769	From you (sing)	مِن لَّدُنكَ
770	From us	مِّن لَّدُنَّآ
771	To us, near us, we have	لَدَيْنَا
772	With them, near them, they have	لَدَيْهِمْ
773	Language, tongue, mouth piece	لِسَان
774	Their languages, their tongues	اَلْسِنَتُهُم
775	The gracious, the kind (Allah)	اَللَّطِيف
776	They play or will play	يَلْعَبُونَ
777	Perhaps I	لَعَلِّيٓ
778	He cursed them	لَعَنَهُم
779	The nonsense, the meaning-less	اَللَّغْو
780	They threw	اَلْقَوْا
781	Fell, thrown unto, been set upon	اُلْقِيَ

782	(Child's) play, sport, distraction, entertainment, fun	لَهْوٌ
783	How I wish	لَيْتَنِي
784	I am not	لَسْتُ
785	You (sing) are not	لَسْتَ
786	Night, nightly	لَيْلًا
787	Night, one night	لَيْلَةٌ
788	One hundred	مِائَةٌ
789	You enjoy (imp,pl)	تَمَتَّعُوا
790	When, at what time, how long?	مَتَىٰ
791	Like you (pl), similar to you	مِثْلُكُمْ
792	Like us, same as us, similar to us	مِثْلُنَا
793	Like (it, her) same as (her, it)	مِثْلَهَا
794	Like them, similar to them	مِثْلُهُمْ

795 Individual, person	اَمْرِئُ
796 His wife	اِمْرَاَتَهُ
797 Twice	مَرَّتَيْنِ
798 Ill (pl), sick (people), sick persons	مَرْضٰى
799 Doubt, dispute, argument	مِرْيَةٍ
800 Touched, befallen, hit	مَسَّ
801 Touched him, befell on him	مَسَّهُ
802 They walk or will walk	يَمْشُوْنَ
803 He walks or will walk	يَمْشِيْ
804 We showered (rain), poured out rain	اَمْطَرْنَا
805 With us	مَعَنَا
806 They played trick, plotted	مَكَرُوْا
807 They play trick or will play, they plot	يَمْكُرُوْنَ
808 Trick, plot	مَكْرُ

809	Their trick	مَكْرُهُمْ
810	His chiefs, council of elders, assembly, audience	مَلَإِيْهٖ
811	I do not posess power or will not	لَآ أَمْلِكُ
812	He posesses power or will posess	يَمْلِكُ
813	His angels	مَلٰٓئِكَتِهٖ
814	He benefitted, he was gracious	مَنَّ
815	The abode, the place of rest, the resting place	اَلْمِهَادُ
816	They died	مَاتُوْا
817	We died	مِتْنَا
818	He dies or will die	يَمُوْتُ
819	He kills or will kill, he causes death	يُمِيْتُ
820	Dead, deadly	مَيْتًا
821	The wave, the surge, the sea	اَلْمَوْجُ

822	Wealth, property, money	مَالًا
823	His wealth, property, money	مَالَهُ
824	I inform you (pl) or will inform	أُنَبِّئُكُمْ
825	He informs you (pl) or will inform	يُنَبِّئُكُمْ
826	He informs them or will inform them	يُنَبِّئُهُمْ
827	Prophet	نَبِيًّا
828	The prophets	اَلْاَنْبِيَاءُ
829	The prophethood	اَلنُّبُوَّةُ
830	We caused to grow	اَنْبَتْنَا
831	The stars	اَلنُّجُوْمُ
832	We saved	نَجَّيْنَا
833	We saved him	نَجَّيْنٰهُ

834	Save me	نَجِّنِي
835	We saved him	فَأَنْجَيْنٰهُ
836	The whispering, the secret conversation	اَلنَّجْوٰى
837	Date, palm	نَخِيل
838	Equal, alike	اَنْدَادًا
839	Repentants, regretting, those who regret	نٰدِمِين
840	He warns or will warn	★ يُنْذِر
841	Give warning (Imp, sing)	★ أُنْذِرِ
842	The warning	★ اَلنُّذُر
843	Warning	★ نُذُر
844	One who warns	★ مُنْذِر
845	Those who warn	★ مُنْذِرِيْن
846	Those who are warned	★ اَلْمُنْذَرِيْن
847	Was revealed	نُزِّلَ

848	Was revealed (fem)	أُنْزِلَتْ
849	Entertaimment, descending place	نُزُلًا
850	Your (pl) wives, your women	نِسَآئِكُمْ
851	He forgot	نَسِيَ
852	He evolved you, originated you, created you	أَنْشَأَكُمْ
853	We evolved, originated, created	أَنْشَأْنَا
854	Fate, share, part (subj)	نَصِيْبٌ
855	Fate, share, part (obj)	نَصِيْبًا
856	He helps you (pl) or will help you	يَنْصُرُكُمْ
857	Those who help, protect	نٰصِرِيْنَ
858	Those who help, helpers, followers, spouses	أَنْصَارٌ
859	Half	نِصْفٌ
860	He sees or will see	يَنْظُرُ

861	They see or will see	يَنْظُرُوْا
862	You see (Imp, pl)	اُنْظُرُوْا
863	They will not be seen (affectionately), they will not be respited	لَا يُنْظَرُوْنَ
864	You wait (Imp, pl)	اِنْتَظِرُوْآ
865	Those who see	اَلنّٰظِرِيْنَ
866	Those who are respited, those who are seen	اَلْمُنْظَرِيْنَ
867	He blessed, graced, granted	اَنْعَمَ
868	You blessed, graced	اَنْعَمْتَ
869	I blessed, graced	اَنْعَمْتُ
870	His blessing, grace	نِعْمَتَهٗ
871	My blessing	نِعْمَتِيَ
872	Will be blown, blown	نُفِخَ
873	The selves	★ اَلْاَنْفُس
874	It benefits or will benefit	يَنْفَعُ

875	Benefit, beneficially, usefully	نَفْعًا	
876	Benefits	مَنَافِع	
877	You (pl) spend or will spend	تُنْفِقُوْا	★
878	He spends or will spend	يُنْفِق	★
879	You (pl) spend (Imp)	اَنْفِقُوْا	★
880	The hypocrites (fem)	اَلْمُنٰفِقٰت	★
881	The hypocrites (masc)	اَلْمُنٰفِقُوْن	★
882	We took revenge	اِنْتَقَمْنَا	
883	They forbid or will forbid	يَنْهَوْنَ	
884	They were forbidden	نُهُوْا	
885	Light (Divine), bright light	نُوْرًا	
886	The she camel	اَلنَّاقَة	
887	They migrated	هَاجَرُوْا	★

888	The migrants, the immigrants	★ اَلْمُهٰجِرِيْنَ
889	He guided you (pl)	★ هَدٰىكُمْ
890	He guided us	★ هَدٰىنَا
891	You (sing) guide or will guide	★ تَهْدِيْ
892	He gives guidance or will give, he guides	★ يَهْدِ
893	He guides them or will guide them	★ يَهْدِيْهِمْ
894	He who got guidance	★ مَنِ اهْتَدٰى
895	So that you may get guidance	★ لَعَلَّكُمْ
896	He who guides, a guide	★ هَادٍ
897	Better guided, more rightly guided	★ اَهْدٰى
898	Those who are guided (Subj)	★ مُهْتَدُوْنَ
899	Those who are guided (obj)	★ اَلْمُهْتَدِيْنَ

900	The animal to be sacrificed	اَلْهَدْىَ ★
901	We destroyed them	اَهْلَكْنٰهُمْ
902	Name of the advisor of Pharoah of Egypt (Hāman)	هَامٰنَ
903	Name of prophet, Hud, jews	هُوْدًا
904	His desire (selfish)	هَوٰىهُ
905	Their promise, their covenant.	مِيْثَاقَهُمْ
906	He got	وَجَدَ
907	I get or will get	اَجِدُ
908	You (pl) get or will get, you find or will find	تَجِدُوْا
909	He gets or will get	يَجِدُ
910	They get or will get	يَجِدُوْا
911	Your (sing) face	وَجْهَكَ
912	Your (pl) faces	وُجُوْهَكُمْ

913	Alone, lonely, He alone, He by Himself, only	وَحْدَهُ
914	One, alone	وَاحِدًا
915	He inspired, revealed	اَوْحٰى
916	He wishes or will wish, desires	يَوَدُّ
917	Love, compassion	مَوَدَّةً
918	Valley, river valley	وَادٍ
919	Leave them (Imp, sing)	ذَرْهُمْ
920	It bears or will bear (responsibility)	تَزِرُ
921	Burden, weight, load, sin, (responsibility)	وِزْرَ
922	One who bears, laden	وَازِرَةٌ
923	The scale, the balance, the measure, the justice, the equity	اَلْمِيْزَانُ
924	His weights, measures	مَوَازِيْنُهُ

925	Its capacity	وُسْعَهَا
926	One who widens Wide, spacious	وَاسِع
927	They narrate or will narrate, portray, describe	يَصِفُونَ
928	We enjoined, we exhorted, advised	وَصَّيْنَا
929	They enjoin or will enjoin	تَوَاصَوْا
930	Will, instruction, order, command	وَصِيَّة
931	He promises you or will promise	يَعِدُكُم
932	Promise	وَعْدًا
933	His promise	وَعْدَهُ
934	The promised time or place, promise, the appointed time	اَلْمِيعَاد
935	Admonition, advice	مَوْعِظَة
936	He fulfills His promise to them, or will fulfill	يُوَفِّيهِم

937	Happened, fell, occured, took place	وَقَعَ
938	That which will happen, real, factual, actual	وَاقِع
939	He abstained, preserved, safe-guarded, protested, feared Allah	* اِتَّقٰى
940	He abstains or will abstain, protects, guards	* يَتَّقِ
941	To fear Allah, you (pl) fear (Imp)	* وَاتَّقُوْنِ
942	The pious, those who ab-stain, The God-fearing ones	* اَلْمُتَّقُوْن
943	Those reclining, leaning	مُتَّكِئِيْن
944	I trusted, relied, depended	تَوَكَّلْتُ
945	They trust	يَتَوَكَّلُوْنَ
946	Put your (sing) trust	تَوَكَّلْ
947	He causes to enter	يُوْلِجُ
948	Their children	اَوْلَادُهُمْ
949	The parents	اَلْوَالِدَيْن

950	His parents	وَالِدَيْهِ
951	Children	الْوِلْدَانِ
952	They turned (their backs)	وَلَّوْا
953	You (pl) turned (your back)	تَوَلَّيْتُمْ
954	You (pl) turned	تَوَلَّوْا
955	You (sing) turn (Imp)	تَوَلَّ
956	The friend, the supporter, the guardian	★ الْمَوْلٰى
957	Your friend, your supporter	★ مَوْلٰىكُمْ
958	We granted, we bestowed	وَهَبْنَا
959	You (sing) grant, you bestow (Imp)	هَبْ
960	Our grief, our woe, woe to us	وَيْلَنَآ
961	The orphan	الْيَتِيْمِ

962	Hand	يَدٌ
963	Your (sing) hand	يَدَكَ
964	His hand	يَدَهٗ
965	Both hands	يَدَيْ
966	My hands	اَيْدِيْ
967	Ease, relief	يُسْرًا
968	Easy, ordinary, little, small	يَسِيْر
969	Easy	يَسِيْرًا
970	The faith, the belief, the certainty	اَلْيَقِيْن
971	The river, the sea	اَلْيَم
972	Your right hand	يَمِيْنِك
973	The oath, the swearing	اَلْاَيْمَان
974	The jews	اَلْيَهُوْد
975	Your (pl) day	يَوْمِكُمْ
976	Their day	يَوْمِهِمْ

List of important, connecting words of the Quran.

1	For, on be half of, to, because of	لِ
2	Not, no, there is no	لَا
3	That, that one	ذٰلِكَ
4	All these	هٰٓؤُلَآءِ
5	Definite article (as the)	اَلْ
6	In it, wherein	فِيْهِ
7	And, and also, with, while, at, by (oath)	وَ
8	Out of what	مِمَّا
9	Them	هُمْ هِمْ
10	What, are not	مَا
11	From, of, some, some of, part of	مِنْ
12	On, upon, on top of, above, over, at	عَلٰى
13	Verily, that, since, because, truly	اِنَّ اَنَّ
14	Whether	ءَ اَ
15	Or, whether	اَمْ

16	Not	لَمْ
17	One who	مَنْ
18	Except, unless, not until	إِلَّا
19	So	فَ
20	When, of	إِذَا
21	Beware, verily, truly, indeed	أَلَا
22	But, however, yet	لٰكِنْ
23	As, like	كَمَا
24	Toward, to, up to, as far as, till, until	إِلَىٰ
25	Surely we	إِنَّا
26	You (possessive) as, like, your	كَ
27	So, when	فَلَمَّآ
28	Or	أَوْ
29	If	لَوْ

30	Yours (pl)	كُمْ
31	You (pl)	اَنْتُمْ
32	If, it is	اِنْ
33	Never, not (in future)	لَنْ
34	This	هٰذَا
35	These	اُولٰٓئِكَ
36	So	اَنْ
37	But	اَمَّا
38	Then, later	ثُمَّ
39	If	اِمَّا
40	Which	لِمَا
41	There	هُنَالِكَ

List of Quranic Terms

1 اَلْاٰخِرَةُ

2 اَلْاِلٰهُ

3 اَلْاِيْمَانُ

4 اَلتِّلَاوَة

5 اَلتَّيَمُّم

6 اَلثَّوَاب

7 اَلْجِهَاد

8 اَلْحَجُّ

9 اَلْحَرَامُ

10 اَلْحُزْن

11 اَلْاِحْسَانُ

12 اَلْمُحْكَمُ

13 اَلْحَلَالُ

14 اَلْحَمْدُ

15 اَلدِّيْنُ

16 اَلرُّبُوْبِيَّة

17 اَلرِّسَالَة

18 اَلزَّكٰوة

19 اَلتَّسْبِيْحُ

20 اَلْاِسْلَامُ

21 اَلْمُتَشَابَهَ

22 اَلشَّرِيْعَةُ

23 اَلشِّرْكُ

24 اَلشَّفَاعَةُ

25 اَلصَّلٰوةُ

26 اَلصَّوْمُ

27 اَلْعِبَادَةُ

28 اَلْعَدْلُ

29 اَلْعَاقِبَةُ

30 اَلْفَرْضُ

31 اَلْفُجُوْرُ

32 اَلْفِسْقُ

33 اَلْقَلْبُ

34 اَلْقِيٰمَةِ

35 اَلْكُفْرُ

36 اَلْمَلٰٓئِكَةِ

37 اَلتَّقْوٰى

List of representative words of the Quran

1 اَلْاَذَانُ

2 اَلْاِمَامَةُ

3 اَلْاُمَّةُ

4 اَلْاَمْرُ بِالْمَعْرُوْفِ

5 اَهْلُ الْبَيْتِ

6 اَلْاٰيَةُ

7 اَلْبِدْعَةُ

8, 9 اَلْبِشَارَةُ وَالنَّذَارَةُ

10 اَلْبَلٰغُ

11 اَلْاِتِّبَاعُ

12 اَلتَّوْبَةُ

13 اَلْجَزَآءُ

14,15 اَلْجَنَّةُ وَالنَّارُ

16 اَلْحَدِيْثُ

17 اَلْحِسَابُ

18 اَلْحَشْرُ

19, 20 اَلْحَقُّ وَالْبَاطِلُ

21	اَلْحِكْمَةَ
22	اَلْخِلَافَت
23,24	اَلْخَوارِق وَالاستدراج
25	اَلذِّكْرُ
26	اَلرُّوْحُ
27	اَلسَّجْدَة
28	اَلسُّنَّةُ
29	اَلشَّيْطٰن
30	اَلشَّهَادَةُ
31	اَلصَّبْرُ
32	اَلصَّدَقٰتُ
33	اَلصِّرَاط الْمُسْتَقِيْمُ
34,35	اَلْاِصْلَاحُ وَالْفَسَادُ
36	اَلطَّهَارَةُ
	اَلظُّلْمُ
38	اَلْمُعْجِزَةُ
39	اَلْعَذَابُ
40	اَلْعَمَلُ

41 اَلْاِسْتِعَاذَةُ

42 اَلْمَغْفِرَةُ

43 اَلْغَيْبِ

44 اَلْفِتْنَةُ

45 اَلْفَلَاحُ

46 اَلْقَدْرُ

47,48 اَلْقُرْاٰنَ وَالْفُرْقَانَ

49 اَلْكِتٰبُ

50 اَلْمَشِيْئَةُ

51 اَلنَّفْسُ

52 اَلْمُنٰفِقُ

53 اَلْهِجْرَةُ

54,55 اَلْهِدَايَةُ وَالضَّلَالُ

56 اَلنَّهْيُ عَنِ الْمُنْكَرِ

57 اَلتَّوْحِيْدُ

58 اَلتَّوْفِيْقَا

59 اَلْوَلِيُّ

60 اُوْلِی الْاَمْرِ

61,62 اَلْوَحْیُ وَالْاِلْهَامُ

Selected Proverbs from the Quran

1 Allah encompasses the Kafirs (disbelievers)

وَاللّٰهُ مُحِيْطٌۢ بِالْكٰفِرِيْنَ

2 Truly Allah is powerful over everything

اِنَّ اللّٰهَ عَلٰى كُلِّ شَيْءٍ قَدِيْرٌ

3 So remember me, I will remember you.

فَاذْكُرُوْنِيْٓ اَذْكُرْكُمْ

4 Allah is with the Sabreen (those who have patience)

اِنَّ اللّٰهَ مَعَ الصّٰبِرِيْنَ

5 Surely you (Oh Prophet of Islam) are of a grand character

وَ اِنَّكَ لَعَلٰى خُلُقٍ عَظِيْمٍ

6 Mischief making is worse than slaughter

وَالْفِتْنَةُ أَشَدُّ مِنَ الْقَتْلِ

7 There is no compulsion in religion

لَآ إِكْرَاهَ فِي الدِّيْنِ

8 Allah never burdens any soul beyond its capacity

لَا يُكَلِّفُ اللّٰهُ نَفْسًا إِلَّا وُسْعَهَا

9 Every soul (life) shall taste death

كُلُّ نَفْسٍ ذَآئِقَةُ الْمَوْتِ

10 Allah is sufficient as Trustee (or guardian)

وَكَفٰى بِاللّٰهِ وَكِيْلًا

11 And that man shall have nothing other than what he strives for

لَّيْسَ لِلْإِنْسَانِ إِلَّا مَا سَعٰى

12 Every thing (in the universe) shall face extinction

كُلُّ مَنْ عَلَيْهَا فَانٍ

13 None will touch it except the pure (at heart)

لَّا يَمَسُّهُۥٓ إِلَّا ٱلْمُطَهَّرُونَ

14 Surely we belong to Allah and to Him we will surely return

إِنَّا لِلَّهِ وَإِنَّآ إِلَيْهِ رَٰجِعُونَ

15 And in their wealth there was a right for the beggar (who asks) and the person who did not ask.

وَفِىٓ أَمْوَٰلِهِمْ حَقٌّ لِّلسَّآئِلِ وَٱلْمَحْرُومِ

16 And hold fast all of you together the rope of Allah and be not divided.

وَٱعْتَصِمُوا۟ بِحَبْلِ ٱللَّهِ جَمِيعًا وَلَا تَفَرَّقُوا۟

17 We are nearer to him than (his) jugular vein

وَنَحْنُ أَقْرَبُ إِلَيْهِ مِنْ حَبْلِ ٱلْوَرِيدِ

18 Verily noblest (most honourable) of you in the sight of Allah is he who is best in conduct (who is pious)

إِنَّ أَكْرَمَكُمْ عِندَ اللَّهِ أَتْقَـٰكُمْ ط

19 Is the reward of Ehsan (goodness) any other than Ehsan?

هَلْ جَزَآءُ الْإِحْسَانِ إِلَّا الْإِحْسَانُ

20 Whosoever is guided is guided only for the (the good of) his own soul (Nafs)

فَمَنِ اهْتَدٰى فَإِنَّمَا يَهْتَدِي لِنَفْسِهٖ ج

21 The Believers are but a single Brotherhood.

إِنَّمَا الْمُؤْمِنُونَ إِخْوَةٌ

The Project

The understanding of the Quran presents a challenge to the non-Arabic knowing believers.

In view of the limitations of the translations the only alternative appear, in the first instance, to learn Arabic. This is, however, not practicable.

The way out has been presented under Dr. Ahmed's well thoughtout Project, the salient features of which are:

A. The basic concept of education has been applied to the study of the Quran and frequently used words of the Quran have been presented.

b. The Terms and Representative words of the Quran have been identified and their meaning have been elucidated through explanatory notes.

c. 467 selected Favorites of the Quran have been presented with English rendering.

This is the first step towards the understanding of the Quran and makes a real beginning to such an approach.

This is yet one more—and most effective—effort in building bridges between the non-Arabic reader and the text of the Quran.

AN EASY WAY TO

THE UNDERSTANDING
of
THE QURAN

Part II

Dr. Hasanuddin Ahmed

KITAB BHAVAN
New Delhi-110002

KITAB BHAVAN
Publishers, Distributors, Exporters & Importers
1784, Kalan Mahal, Darya Ganj,
New Delhi - 1100 02 (India)

Phones	:	(91-11) 23277392/93, 23274686, 32906494
Fax	:	(91-11) 23263383
Website	:	www.kitabbhavan.com
Email	:	nasri@vsnl.com
	:	nusrat@bol.net.in

ISBN : 81-7151-100-7 (PB) Set
ISBN : 81-7151-102-3 (Vol. II)

Printed & Published in India by :
Nusrat Ali Nasri for KITAB BHAVAN
1784, Kalan Mahal, Darya Ganj,
New Delhi - 1100 02 [India]

TABLE OF CONTENTS

AN EASY WAY TO THE UNDERSTANDING OF THE QURAN

1. INTRODUCTION

In the first part two lists of the frequently used words of the *Quran* were presented. Now we are happy to present the explanatory notes on the terms and the representative words of the *Quran* and the selected *Quranic* proverbs with English rendering. It is hoped that this part will be received with the same enthusiasm as the first.

The one and the only aim of the project is to make the understanding of the *Quran* easy for such people whose mother tongue is not Arabic.

2. THE *QURAN*

Quran is the Book from *Allah* for the guidance of mankind. This Book is easy to understand. Everyone can and has to study it through self effort. The guidance of a qualified teacher, however, will always be useful. When the *Quran* is approached objectively and with an open mind *Allah* will grant to the sincere inquirer knowledge of the universal guidance; for the *Quran* has stratification of meaning (having many levels or layers of meaning). The *Quran* meets its reader at his own level of comprehension and reveals its meaning to him according to his intelligence and intellectual capacity. The *Quran* rivets the sincere reader's attention and when one reads it carefully, it influences profoundly.

The *Quranic* truths have come down to us with pellucid clarity. There is no ambiguity in the *Quran*. There is no secret, hidden or underlying meaning of the *Quran* or any part thereof. The message of the *Quran* is accessible to one and all.

It is a well known fact that there has been no change of a single word or syllable in the text of the *Quran*. There is only one text of the *Quran* in circulation today and it is exactly the same which the Prophet of Islam (PBUH) had received from *Allah* and handed down to the posterity through his companions. In other words the *textus receptus* of the *Quran* in today's world is the exact *textus originales*.

One impoprtant point needs clarification. All the 114 Surah of the *Quran* and the *Ayat* in every Sura had been arranged and recorded in writing during the lifetime of the Prophet (PBUH) under his personal directions. The arrangement is not haphazard or arbitrary as often suggested by western scholars. Close study reveals a unique and planned sequence. The *Quran* possesses a thematic and aesthetic unity, its own ethos and a style that is unparallelled.

The *Quran* is divided into Ayat or divisions losely called verses in English. The end of Ayat is determined by the position of a small circle such as O. The early Muslims did not agree as to the position of these circles and so the number of divisions differ in the following five editions.

1. Kufah. The Muslims of kufah were followers of Ali son of Abu Talib. Their way of reckoning is generally adopted in India. They reckon 6236 Ayat.

2. Basrah. The Muslims of Basrah follow the order of Asim son of Hajjaj, one of the earliest converts of Islam. According to this arrangement there are 6216 Ayat.

3. Shami. The Muslims of Sham (Syria) followed Abdullah son of Umar, one of the earliest converts. They reckon 6250 Ayat.

4. Makkah. According to this arrangement there are 6212 Ayat.

5. Madina. This way of reading contains 6214 Ayat.

The variation in the number of Ayat is also due to the fact that some have counted Bismilla-h-irRehman nir-Rahim as part of Surah and others have not.

The diversity of punctuation does not, however, affect the contents of the *Quran*.

The Ayat or divisions of the Quran are not necessarily sentences. The *Quran* is divided into divisions (mostly according to the rhymed word endings). If there is a pause due to recurrence of co-sounding endings the division usually terminates. The sentence may or may not coterminate with the Ayat. 1

The main reason why the *Quran* was revealed in stages over a period of 23 years and not in one single revelation was to gradually implement the laws of *Allah* and to make understanding, implementation and memorization of the revelations easier for the Muslims.

In the *Quran* there is no incongruity in style, no gap in the continuity of thought and no lack of interconnection between various subjects. The *Quran* is not irrelevant anywhere with regard to its main theme. Every topic revolves around the main theme which serves as the guidance to mankind.

There is no repetition in the *Quran* as alleged by some Orientalists. Repitition is defined as that which does not contain any additional benefit. The frequency of the Ayat (Q55:13), is thirty one times but in every occurance the implication and connotation is different. The same is the case with other Ayat or words which occur many a time. The purpose is to clarify the meanings of concepts and the terms of the *Quran* or to lay stress on certain teachings; but as far as the meanings are concerned we can safely assert that there is no repetition.

Many derogatory remarks have been made by some western scholars, wilfully or out of ignorance but the *Quran* is a solid anvil on which many critical hammers have been broken.

----

1. Both Mohammad Marmaduke Pickthall in his Introduction to "The Meaning Of The Glorous Koran" and A. Yusuf Ali in his introductory note "Divisions of the *Quran*", in his English translation of "The Holy *Quran*" have also expressed similar views.

Idolatory is mostly misunderstood and misinterpreted by some Muslims. Idolatory is the subject matter of the *Quran* and its various aspects are profoundly discussed throughout the *Quran*. For the clear understanding of the *Quran* it is necessary to know the exact nature of idolatory in the Arab society at the advent of Islam. It will guide the Muslims to avoid Shirk prevelant in some Muslim societies.

Allah was regarded by the Arabs as one God. Kaabah was called the House of *Allah*. The objects of worship were a number of Idols which were called daughters of *Allah* and intercessors. The Idols were worshipped by individual preferences or family affiliations.

Quran is a book that has produced a community, given rise to a culture and a civilization and has changed the course of human history leaving a most profound influence upon it.

The *Quran* by acclamation was up to the standard of the Arabs, the most outstanding masterpiece of literature.

3. THE UNDERSTANDING

It is the duty of every Muslim not only to acquire the understanding of the *Quran* for himself but to evolve methods of making the understanding easy for others - Muslims and non Muslims. One aspect of this great task is to take the first step towards the easy understanding of the *Quran*.

"The one prerequisite for understanding the Quran is to study it with an open and detached mind...... one should free the mind of bias in favor or against it, get rid of all preconceived opinions and then approach it with the sole desire of understanding it".1

4. WHAT IS A TERM?

If a word is used in special sense and if it pertains to any discipline of letters it is called a term.

---

1. S. Maududi, An Introduction To *Quran*, Unity Publishing Company, Iowa.

When a science, philosophy or thought is developed or when new ideas for social reforms are introduced, the ordinary words prevalent are not sufficent and capable to express the specifically developed units of thought of that particular discipline. As such either new words are coined or the ordinary words are chosen and special meanings are assigned to them. In other words a new status is given to the ordinary words of the language. When a word becomes a term it loses its original dictionary meaning and assumes a new meaning and a new status. Terms are in reality hints which turn the mind towards the cluster (group) of thought and idea they contain.

Thus a term, as distinct from a word, is an expression that has a precise meaning in some uses. It is peculiar to a particular science or discipline. It conveys a full thought. Term is the basis on which exchange of thought is possible. "If you wish to converse with me", said Voltair, "define your terms".

Just as letters are necessary for words, and words are required to make up sentences, in the same manner terms are inevitable for any discipline. For every art or discipline, for every philosophy or ideology, there are particular terms through which the meaning and connotations are explained and elucidated.

5. *QURANIC* TERMS

As mentioned above a major problem with every new revolutionary movement is its nomenclature. The *Quran* is not only a representative book of a dynamic movement but it is preeminently *Al Hikmat*, a Book of Wisdom. As in the case of any discipline, the *Quran* has also a system of terms. There are many words which have been used in some special sense quite different from their ordinary connotation; such as Al-Ilah (7), Al-Ibadat(27), Al-Deen(15) etc. Each term encompasses a whole concept. It is imperative to know these terms to grasp the spirit of the *Quran*. In the *Quran* not less than thirty seven terms have been used. In a religion that sparkles with new ideas and new concepts in a short span of time, such as Islam, terms and concepts play an important role. The new dynamic religion was taught through the *Quran*, which had its own unique language and terminology. The terms of the *Quran* in the first place have been picked up from the Urf (prevalent or current vocabulary) and then special meanings have been assigned to them. "There is a repertory of familiar themes running through the whole Koran; each Sura elaborates or adumbrates one or more-often many-of these;" 1. These *Quranic* themes or concepts expressed through *Quranic* terms were the force that have shaped the minds of the early converts and these concepts are still capable to shape the minds of Muslims of today and tomorrow until posterity, if the *Quranic* terminology is fully and correctly comprehended. The serious reader of the *Quran* must be prepared to absorb as readily as possible a whole range of new concepts and terms. Without the full grasp of the teminology of the *Quran* all the efforts to understand Islam will be futile. One cannot expect to profit seriously .from the *Quranic* teachings. The thought of the *Quran* cannot be deeply shared without getting acquainted with ideas of which there is no exact equivalent. in any language.

In order to understand the *Quran* a clear comprehension of the full connotation of these terms is a *sine qua non.* These terms are fully explained by the *Quran* itself. The Prophet of Islam [PBUH] also explained these terms to his followers, but in later centuries mostly due to the influences of Sufism and of alien civilizations their meaning mostly slipped away from the Muslim mind and changes crept in. Thus every term was expanded in its connotation and became elastic to accomodate the new trends of thought relating to that term.2 For example the term Al-Ihsan(11) or the representative word Al-Zikr[25] assume wider range of meaning in post *Quranic* Sufi literature so much so that today it becomes rather difficult to sift the *Quranic* meaning from the jargon collected around these lofty concepts.

It is necessary to take deliberate and effective steps to understand the meanings of the *Quranic* terms, which are well preserved in the *Quran*.

----

1. Preface to "The Koran interpreted" by A.J. Arberry
2. Maulana Maududi in his Introduction to "The Four Basic Terms of the *Quran*", has also expressed similar views.

6. *QURANIC* TERMS VERSUS TERMS OF OTHER DISCIPLINES

In one respect the nature of the *Quranic* terms is different from the terms of other disciplines. The terms in other disciplines are specific. The *Quran* does not adhere to the term in one form but freely uses their derivatives as synonyms for the terms. For example not less that 18 derivatives of the term Al-Jihad(7) have been used in the *Quran*. Similarly the representative word Al-Balagh[16] has been used with 18 derivatives.

7. REPRESENTATIVE WORDS OF THE *QURAN*

There are certain words in the *Quran* which cannot be treated as terms because their dictionary meaning is retained. Such as Al-Tauba[12], Al-Jaza[13] etc. Yet these are at the same time not the ordinary words. These words play an important role to represent Islam and its teachings.

After the *Quranic* terms the representative words are very important and deserve particular attention.

The difference between the general words and the representative words of the *Quran* should be maintained. For every revolutionary and dynamic movement representative words are important because it is through them that the fundamental principles of the message are explained. The *Quran* also has used its representative words to spread its message.

8. LIMITATIONS OF TRANSLATIONS

Many translations of the *Quran* attempt to provide significantly accurate meaning; yet translations have their own limitations and shortcomings. However successful a translation may be, it cannot convey the original sense and impression and it can never be perfect. The masterpiece of a language cannot be rendered in purity and precision in other languages. Every language has its own spirit and ethos. The nuances of thought and delicate shades of meanings and ideas, depth of feelings and sensivity of impressions cannot be conveyed with the self same characteristics of style and diction as in the original.

Translations therefore, have this inherent weakness of imperfection. Attempt to translate the untranslatable *Quranic* terms and representative words may be futile and suffer from an additional handicap as they represent human efforts to translate the divine word into worldly languages.

As in the case of terms of any sciene or discipline the terms of the *Quran* are obsolutely untranslatable. No human language can possibly be adequate for the highest spiritual thought. A shade of the meaning conveying the sense only in part can be expressed in a nearly equivalent word of other language. Thus if the terms or the representative words of the *Quran* are translated, in effect it amounts to fossilisation of the partly conveyed meaning.

No matter how hard the translator tries, his achievement will fall short of his estimation and will hardly do justice to the original text of the *Quran*.

There cannot be one single word in any language to convey the meaning of a *Quranic* term. A group of words however, can give some idea of a terms. In other words explanatory notes are required to convey the real meaning of the term.

Quranic term is a full ray of light; when a translater looks at it through the prism of an imperfect equivalent or a modern analytical language, he misses a great deal of its meaning by confining his attention to one particular tinge.

In the Salat the recitation of the original text of the *Quran* is obilgatory for the Muslims all over the world. The Muslims are therefore, very close to the original text of the *Quran*. This has many advantages. It is one of the bases of the Muslim brotherhood. Introduction of the practice of retaining in every language, the *Quranic* terms in their original prestine purity will further strengthen the unity of Muslim Ummah.

When the *Quran* was translated, they tried to translate along with the text, the terms and the representative words and little attention was paid to bring out the sense in which they were used. For example the term Salat(25) has been translated in English as prayers, worship etc.

Even the proper noun for the Almighty has been translated. *Allah* and God or *Allah* and Lord are popularly considered as synonyms but in fact they are not. *Allah* is the proper noun as against the attributes which are actually more than the generally accepted 99. We never translate a name from one language to another. Why then the name of the Almighty be translated? Whatever the language the name *Allah* should be retained. Moreover the word God carries in it in one way or the other the concept of father in the Biblical sense.

Mohd Marmaduke Pickthall in his English translation of the *Quran* "The Meaning of the Glorious Koran" says:

> "I have retained the word *Allah* throughout because there is no corresponding word in English. The word *Allah* has neither feminine nor plural and has never been applied to anything other than the unimagine-able Supreme Being. I use the word God only where the corresponding word ilah is found in the Arabic".

It is one of the merits of the *Quran* that it explains and elucidates its own terms. As such any attempt to translate the terms and the representative words or to try to find the equivalent is undesireable if not futile. Whichever the language into which the *Quran* is being translated or explained the terminology should be left untampered.

9. EXPLANATORY NOTES

The explanatory notes presented in this volume consist of concise and basic information. Far from being the last word, these are only the first step. These may be regarded as key-note data. The readers are advised to prepare their own notes and make constant effort to increase their knowledge on the real concept of every term and the representative word of the *Quran*.

Wherever the Terms are referred to in the preface or in the explanatory notes, serial numbers are given in small brackets for every term. Similarly the serial numbers of the Representative words are given in square brackets.

The terms and the Representative words are presented in Arabic and the transliteration in Roman script.

10. SOURCES

In preparing the explanatory notes material has been drawn from the following among others:

(a) Notes by A. Yusuf Ali included in his Translation of The Holy Quran.

(b) Shorter Encyclopaedia of Islam. Edited on Behalf of the Royal Netherlands Academy By H.A.R. Gibb and J.H, Kramers

(c) Dictionary of Islam By Thomas Patrick Hughes. Islamic Book Publishers P.O.Box 20210 Safat, Kuwait.

(d) Various writings of Maulana Maududi

(e) Various writings of Dr. Muhammad Hamidullah.

(f) Islam-Belief And Teachings. By Ghulam Sarwar.

(g) Ulumul *Quran*. By Ahmed Von Denffer

(h) Various writings of A.S. Hashim M.D.

(i) Various writings of Dr. Mirza Abul Fazl.

11. WHAT IS A PROVERB?

A proverb, maxim or aphorism is a short concisely expressed principle, rule of conduct or a statement of general and well known self evident fact in common use, expressed in appropriate and effective language. It is a proposition whose truth is so evident at first sight that no process of reasoning or demonstration can make it plainer. It is a pithy, terse and pointed expression in a single sentence containing some important precept, or truth acceptable to one and all. It is a brief reflection of plain, wise saying, short instructive remark or rule of conduct that sinks into heart.

12. *QUARANIC* FAVORITES

With a strong conviction that the *Quranic* proverbs will be of immense value in the quest for the easy understanding of the *Quran* an anthology of 467 *Quranic* proverbs with English translation are being presented in this volume. The selection is not complete and exhaustive. It is however fairly representative.

Quran is like an ocean which abounds in various types of jewels and treasures. These are the essence of the *Quran*, its heart, its pith and its profound excellence.

There is not to be found in any composition of world literature an aphorism more eminently distinguished by profound and serene wisdom, than the *Quranic* gems.

Quranic proverbs are intended to approach the human problem with stark realism. The reader will find in these proverbs echo of the moral values that stirred his own soul.

Humanity today is groping in the dark. There is universal demand for guidance. The *Quranic* proverbs are a response to the quest of the mind afflicted by worries and miseries. These proverbs are a dynamic and safe anchor for humanity, the embodiments of eternal values necessary for the individual and the community.

The *Quranic* proverbs can be classified into moral social, religious and political maxims that solve the problems which confront humanity in their day to day life.

The Muslim mind today is also searching for the light in which they can venture to advance united into a glorious future. The *Quranic* proverbs aim to revive the ethical standard and elevate the levels set by the preachings of earlier Prophets under the guidance of *Allah* .These proverbs are pieces of advice one may accept on righteous action and piety.

The teachings enunciated in the *Quranic* proverbs are not dogmatic and rigid but adaptable to all ages. The beautiful gems are intimately connected with the guidance of humanity which is the central theme of the *Quran*. The *Quranic* proverb could easily be used in every day conversation, debates and prudent writings, to be cited in everyday situations.

There was a time when some divisions of the *Quran* became proverbs and were often quoted in daily conversation. Even today the *Quranic* proverbs are admired and quoted by Muslims and non Muslims but to a lesser extent. Now the same *Quranic* gems are being presented with the hope that these gems if learnt by heart will become popular with the Muslims and will again be used as proverbs. It is also hoped that these proverbs will enrich the individual with the knowledge of the *Quran* and will promote familiarity with the *Quran*. If they are learnt during the formative period, they will help in building the mind in conformity with the teachings of the *Quran*.

Presenting a selection of *Quranic* gems apparently implies that the compiler is of the view that some parts of the *Quran* are more remarkable than others. This appears to be anomalous with the fact that the entire *Quran* is the word of *Allah*. How then can one distinguish some parts from the other? The answer is simple: An effort is made to demonstrate the truth of the Saying of the Prophet [PBUH] on the excellence of some of the striking *Ayah* of the *Quran* and on the nobility and specification of some *Ayah*.

The aim is to initiate the readers into moral and social teachings of the Quran and its values.

13. CRITERIA

As beauty cannot be defined by reasoning or in words, the beauty of the gems of the *Quran* can only be felt as joy in the heart or the inner self. One may be able to give numerous reasons to justify the preference given to these selected gems but the common factor in all these gems is beauty that enraptures reason itself.

There are certain portions of the *Quran* which in a short appropriate language tell about the ultimate reality of all things, of the real and final nature of the universe, of mind and the interrelation of mind and matter. These are heads and shoulders above the other portions and the compiler was delighted to pick them up.

If an *ayat* or a part of the *ayat* contained divine names and attributes and if the *ayat* was found more comprehensive of the aims of the *Quran* it was a good reason to say that it deserved preference over other *ayah* and it was thus selected.

If any *ayat* spoke of righteous action and of practical life it was not allowed to escape.

Not many attempts have been made in the past to gather the *Quranic* gems. One such selection is Jawaherul *Quran*. In Jawaherul *Quran*, Al Ghazali has presented the Jewels and the Pearls of the *Quran*. The purpose of the Jewels (763 verses) is, according to Al Ghazali, to gather the light of knowledge (of *Allah*) His attributes and His works. This is the cognitive part. The purpose of the Pearls (741 verses) is to urge man to follow steadfastness on the straight path by action. This is the practical part.[1]

As for the English rendering of the 467 proverbs an effort has been made to employ clear, simple language and distinct English words. In the English renderings, a slight deviation from the existing English translations of the *Quran* will be

----

1. The Jewels of the *Quran* Al Ghazali's Theory By Mohd Abul Quasem 1977).

noticed. In many English translations the influence of the Biblical translation is evident due to which the renderings are not very clear and comprehensible to the general reader.

In translating the 467 proverbs an earnest attempt is made to retain in plain language the original emphasis and force contained in the original text of the selected proverbs.

The reader will notice that present translator mostly agrees with the English translation of the *Quran* by Dr Mirza Abul Fazl to whom he is indebted.

In "The *Quran*: The First American Version", Prof. T. B. Irving has achieved considerable success in making the *Quran* accessible to all American readers, while retaining the aesthetic beauty of the original. It was also found helpful in rendering the proverbs into English.

14. CONCLUSION

The understanding of *AL-Quran* which is very essential for the Muslims, presents a challange to the non-Arabic knowing believers.

Taking for granted the inherent incapabilities and limitations of tranlations and the extent to which these translations can some times create confusion, the only alternative appears in the first instance to learn Arabic, the language of the *Quran*. Maybe, more and more scholars in various parts of the world can be induced and encouraged to learn Arabic, but it is not easy for the non Arabic speaking students to learn the language.

One plausible solution or way out is presented under this project. The salient features of the project are:

(a). To introduce to the beginners frequently used words of the *Quran*.

The two lists (first list of 835 words whose frequency in the *Quran* is 10 and above and the second list of 976 words whose frequency in the *Quran* is 5 to 9) have already been published.

Thus for the first time the basic concept of education ie. introducing to the students the selected vocabulary having high frequency is applied to the study of the *Quran*.

(b). To furnish explanatory notes on the untranslatable *Quranic* terms and representatives words of the *Quran, explanatory notes on the 37 terms and 62 representative words of the Quran* are being presented in this volume.

(c). To acquaint the readers with the *Quranic* proverbs so that they are better placed in the understanding of the *Quran*.

467 *Quranic* proverbs with English rendering are also presented in this volume. Thus the gap for this kind of work has been filled up. It is hoped that this endeavour will stimulate interest in the study of the *Quran* and help readers in its understanding. Eventually performing the Salat in the original text of the *Quran*, will be more meaningful and purposeful.

15. ACKNOWLEDGEMENTS

It is not always easy to acknowledge such assistance as the author had, in preparing the explanatory notes from his esteemed friend Mir Mahmood Ali Khan, who has a zest for a sincere and close study of the Quran. He had the good fortune of assisting Dr. Syed Abdul Lateef in translating the Quran into English. He himself has written a book, "Initiation To The Glorious Quran" which he is trying to publish from the U.S.A.

Deepest appreciation must go to my dear son, Mr. Zaheer Ahmed for providing me all the facilities with great care and devotion which enabled me to complete this part in record time. May Allah bless him.

Before publication this part was also revised by my good friend Dr. Ahmed H. Sakr. Sincere thanks are therefore, due to him.

Thanks are also due to Mr. Mohd. Mazhar Hussaini Secy. Iqra International Educational Foundation for his continued interest in the Project.

It is my earnest prayer that Allah may accept this humble effort and make it useful for an easy understanding of the Quran.

February 12, 1987
2528 Brunswick Cr.
Woodridge, IL 60517

Dr. Hasanuddin Aḥmed

Explanatory Notes on the Terms of the *Quran*

(1) Al-Akhirah الآخِرَة

Akhirah is hereafter, it applies to the next stage of life after death. The idea of Akhirah shows that there is accountability for the human beings. There are moral laws just as the physical laws. According to the *Quran* there is a reward for every human action. If the deed is good the result will be good and vice versa. What shape the good or bad deeds will take cannot be determined by human reason. The mention of this life in the *Quran* is mostly in parables. The activities of the adherents are controlled by this great concept. According to the *Quran* those persons who do good deeds are the people of paradise. The well being and enjoyments of heavenly life are reserved for these people.

According to the *Quran* the human activity is judged according to the intention. Personal gain is regarded as the worldly gain and the collective gain is called the gain of the Akhirah.

Yaumul Aqirah or the last day is another name for the day of judgement.

Belief in the *Akhirah* is one of the basic articles of Faith Iman (3) in Islam (20)

(2) Al-Ilah الْإِلٰه

The literal meaning of Al-Ilah is divinity.

According to the *Quran Al-Ilah* is the being which is beloved, gives peace of mind, which according to the devotee is elevated and exalted; which guards and protects when one is in fear and worry. The being which according to man's belief provides gains and losses, answers prayer and has power over our existence is *Al-Ilah*. Man in his ignorance selects the *Ilah* of his choice, but there is no *Ilah* except *Allah*.

According to the *Quran Allah* alone is Al-Ilah. The prophet of Islam said to Abu Jahal "If you recite one sentence you will become the ruler of Arabia" Abu Jahal replied "if so I can recite ten sentences "The prophet replied " No only one sentence *La Ilaha Il Allah*"1. This shows the importance of assigning all the attributes of Al Ilah exclusively to *Allah*. La Ilaha Il *Allah* None has the right to be worshipped but *Allah* This is the first article of Faith and the first pillar of Islam, declaring the Faith i.e. Iman(1).

(3) Al Iman الإِيمَانُ

Iman means steadfast faith, firm and implicit belief. It is credence, fidelty, allegance or loyalty to a way of life after mature judgement.

"When a particular concept becomes current by virtue of the fact that it attracts attention of the people it becomes a belief. This belief when goes deep and becomes a state of mind and style of life, it is styled as Faith". 2

Iman is peace and reliability. It is trustworthiness, concientiousness and responsible attitude. It is to regard and accept others as peaceful and trustworty and also to be peaceful with others. Iman has vast and collective connotation rather than limited and individual one.

True Iman creates such spiritual power that no worldly power can frighten it.

----

1. It is interesting to note that this sentence in Arabic is comprised of only 3 letters (i.e. ا-ل-ه)

2. Dr. M. Kirmani's Paper Quranic Method of Enquiry in "Quest For New Science".

Iman "is a state of happiness acquired by virtue of positive action and constructive concepts as well as dynamic and effective measures". 1

The *Quran* regards the material and sensual life (like that of the animals) as the way of Kufr(35). The other and higher plane of life is not regarded as the higher form of animal life but the imitation of divine attributes. To have faith in *Allah* implies the acceptance of this higher plane of life. Awareness of wrong and injustice is an important ingredient of Iman. The prophet of Islam (PBUH) said if any impropriety or injustice is committed in your presence remedy it with your hands. If it is not possible (due to strong opposition) then stop it with your tongue. If even that is not possible then realize in your mind that it is wrong. For that is the last stage of Iman.

Following are the five articles which form the foundation for the superstructure of Islam ie. belief in:

1. Allah
2. His Angels
3. His Books
4. His Messengers
5. The Day of Judgement

Mumin is a believer. Al-Muminun is plural of Mumin, The Believer.

(4) Al-Tilawah اَلتِّلَاوَة

Al-Tilawah literally means reading. This term is derived from Tilawa meaning to follow step by step. Al Tilawah is a term exclusively used for the reading or for the recitation of the *Quran*. As the lips move in the recitation of the Quranic words the mind has to ponder over the meaning.

----

1. Hammudah Abdalati: Islam In Focus

(5) Al-Taiyammum التيمم

The dictionary meaning of Al-Taiyammum is intending or proposing. As a term Al-Taiyammum is an act of cleaning the face and both the hands with clean sand or clay when water is not readily available or cannot be used due to a valid reason such as illness. Taiyammum is a concession given for performance of the Salat(25) in time. (Q5:9) "If you cannot find water, then take fine (clean) sand and wipe your faces and your hands therewith. Allah does not wish to make any hinderance for you".

(6) Al-Thawab الثواب

As-Thawab means recompence or reward. "The best awards are from Allah", Q:3195. As-Thawab is the riches of the life of Al-Akhirah (1).

Thawab as a term means the reward for the good deeds. There are certain conditions for getting the reward.

(a). The deed to be performed should be as ordained by *Allah*.
(b). Should be as prescribed by the Prophet.
(c). Should be performed with the sole purpose of pleasing *Allah*.
(d). Should be free from personal motives such as gaining popularity etc.
(e). If the deed is being performed with the use of wealth such wealth should be the acquisition of fair and permitted means.

Even if one condition is not fulfilled there will be no reward. The Thawab has the same significance in Al-Akhirah(1) as the Wealth and other material acquisitions have in this world. The riches in the life of Al-Alkhirat depends on the Thawab which is earned during the worldly life.

(7) Al- Jihad الجهاد

Al-Jihad means an effort or strife. Jihad is an all round struggle in the way of *Allah* i.e. to make *Allah's* word (Al-Islam) superior. Jihad is one of the principles of AlIslam.

It is obligatory for every Muslim to exercise all his powers. It may be in the form of intellectual and physical capacities or the gift of speech or his moral strength courage and steadfastness in the face of hardships and hurdles, for the cause of *Allah*.

The term Jihad is often confused with the word qital (fighting) and these are used in one and he same sense whereas the *Quran* has made a clear distinction between them.

The Prophet of Islam explaining the true qualities of Mujahid (one who makes Jihad) remarked "The Mujahid is one who tries to struggle against his self ie. evil self."

To fight in the cause of Truth is one of the highest form of charity. What can one offer that is more precious than one's life?

The Jihad against the enemies of *Allah* with one's life is only a part of the struggle which a true Muslim carries on for the sake of *Allah*.

"If non Muslims are peaceful with the Muslims or even indifferent to Islam there cannot be any ground or justification to declare war on them. There is no such thing as religious war or to force Islam on non Muslims because if Islam does not emerge from deep convictions from within, it is not acceptable to *Allah*, nor can it help its professors"1

Jihad is spending our lives or the lives of those near and dear to us. It may either be the loss of all the fruits of a life-time labour not only in material goods but in some intellectual or moral gain, some position which seemed in our eyes to be

----

1. Hammudah Abdalati: Islam In Focus.

eminently desirable in itself, but which we must cheerfully sacrifice if necessary for the cause. These extreme sacrifices must be made under the order of the righteous Imam or Ulil Amr[60] who can see the entire perspective and judge justly of their necessity. There is no virtue in mere sacrifice when offered at the whim of an individual. Courage (resistance to the test of fear) and self denial (resistence to the test of Hunger and Desire) also should be displayed under the guidance of the Imam.

(8)Al- Hajj اَلْحَجّ

Hajj is the fifth pillar of Islam. The intention of proceeding to Makkah for performing the traditional pilgrimage is called Hajj. Hajj is obligatory to every Muslim who is of responsible age, in good health and is financially capable of undertaking the journey. Hajj is also obligatory for a Muslim who visits Makkah on the occasion of Hajj. Hajj is obligatory once during a life-time. The course of Hajj is another unique characteristic of Islam. It is an annual conference of Islam Faith where Muslims from all over the world meet and study their common problems. It is a regular convention of peace. In the course of Hajj peace is the dominant theme; Peace with *Allah* and on'es soul, peace with one another and even with all living creatures, animals birds and insects. It is a demonstration of universality of Islam and the brotherhood of Muslims.

(9)Al-Haram اَلْحَرَام

Al-Haram in Arabic means that which is sacred, hollowed, reserved, prohibited, unlawful or forbidden. Haram is punishable from the view point of Islam. Each of the two mosques at Makkah and Medina is called Masjid Al-Haram as these mosques are considered as sacred and it is forbidden to violate their sanctity. The month of Hajj, Zul Hajj was a sacred month in which warfare was prohibited by Arabic custom. The month preceding (zul-qad) and the month following (Muharram) were included in the prohibition.

The uniform dress prescribed at the time of Hajj is called Ihraam as after wearing that dress some of the actions ordinarily allowed are forbidden. Haram also means to abstain. Mahroom is he who is stripped from acquiring the commodities of daily use. As a term Haram as against Halal (13) is that which is forbidden in Islam. One who disregards Haram is regarded as Kafir (35) and who commits what is Haram is considered as Fasiq (32).

(10) Al-Huzn اَلْحُزْنِ

Huzn is opposite of suroor meaning enjoyment. If a man covets and expects for something of his liking and fails to get it he is disappointed. As a term Huzn is dillusionment of those who believe in Ilah other than *Allah* and have the design (Q17:84) Shakila of life other than prescribed by *Allah*.

(11) Al-Ihsan اَلْإِحْسَانِ

Al-Ihsan is to do good to others, confer favors or to perform an action in perfect form. It is the highest form or level of worship. The meaning of this term is to adore *Allah* (with such a devotion) as if you see Him, and if you do not see Him yet He sees you. Ihsan is nothing but the perfectly sincere adoration of *Allah* in performing His worship. Al-Ihsan is therefore, the higher quality of worship; for worship with the feeling that we are in the actual presence of the Almighty will be with more devotion and Solemnity Al-Ihsan not only applies to the Salat(25) or to the other forms of Worship but to all human activity as well. Man should always feel the presence of *Allah*. With that feeling the direction of every human action will be towards a higher goal. The concept of Al-Ihsan is the key to improve the quality of all human activity.

The good deeds performed with the full consciousness of Allah's presence are also called Ihsan. This is in fact the real service to mankind. According to the *Quran*, there is no reward for such actions i.e. Ihsan except Ihsan (Q55:60). This reward is with Allah and it is also obligatory on the recipient of such Ihsan. Mere gratitude for Ihsan is not sufficient. Return of service of similar high quality is necessary.

(12)Al-Muhkam المحكم

As a term Al-Muhkam applies to a set of the Ayat of the *Quran*. Ayat Muhkamaat are those Ayat which contain clear injunctions wherein there is no possibility of any doubt. It is incumbent on every believer i.e. Mummin(3) to strictly follow the commands contained in these Ayat. As against the Ayat Muhkamat, there are Ayat Mutashabihaat(21). Quran calls the Ayah Muhkamat as Ummul Kitab (mother of the book i.e. the essence of the Book).

(13)Al- Halal الحلال

Al-Halal means lawful, permissable or legal. Every thing that is not specifically forbidden in Islam is permissable and it is called halal. Al-Halal is therefore opposite of AlHaram(9)

Animals (other than forbidden) slaughtered with the name of *Allah* as prescribed are called halal.

Man has to be careful about his actions and about his food. "Let man be watchful of his food" 80:24 said the Quran.

(14)Al- Hamd الحمد

Al Hamd means Praise, commitment or obedience. Al-Hamd Lillah means all Praise is due to Him alone to whom every one is duty-bound in submission to His will. In the entire creation of Allah, human beings alone are endowed with the faculty of speech. Hence verbal Praise of Allah is one of the duties, among others, assigned to them.

(15)Al-Din الدين

The term Al Din is used by the *Quran* for religion. The human society deals with the individual, mutual relations and dealings. The system which deals with all the three aspects of socicety according to the *Quran* and which binds us back to *Allah* is called Al-Din. This system can be the right one or the ill fashioned, corrupt one. It can be based on Al-Haqq[19] or on Al-Batil[20].

If in the system the center of loyalty, fidelity, obedience and supplications is *Allah* then this Din will be the right one. If on the contrary the center is other than *Allah* then the Din will be ill fashioned.

All the Rusul (17) who made their appearances from time to time propagated Islam (20). The common teaching of all Rasuls is Al Din.

The *Quran* has not used the word religion for Islam. The *Quran* regards Islam as Din. The system which is employed to use the Din in individual and social life is called Al-Shariat(22). The different interpretations and explanations offered by the scholars of Al-Shariat are the schools of thought. Muslims cannot have their own way in the matter of Din or Shariat. They can however, have their own preferances to the schools of thought or religions. Thus Islam by itself is Din and the school of thought are part of Din.

Other world religions have lost the original divine system. They have changed center of loyalties to beings other than *Allah* and systems other than divine. They have retained certain modes of prayer and religious practices in shape of their religions. In Islam the divine system and the original Din of *Allah* is fully preserved. It is the duty of every Muslim to establish this Din It would be a contradiction if the Muslims while believing in *Allah*'s Din divert their loyalties to beings and systems other than *Allah* and perform the prayer in the limited field of religion.

(16) Al-Rububiah الرُبُوبِيَة

Al-Rububiah is a great attribute of *Allah*. *Allah* is a sustainer of the entire creation. The universe created by *Allah* is in the process of evolution. It is constantly growing into perfection according to *Allah*'s Design. *Allah* is constantly attending to the needs of the universe and the individual needs of the beings of the universe during their evolution and development. Just as a tree from the stage of the seed to the full growth requires constant provision of air light manure and water according to the actual need and requires a systen to look after the individual need with care and affection, the entire universe and every living and non living being also requires an orderly plan. Providing such plan is called Rububiah and the one who provides such sustenance is called Rubb.

Al-Rubb the Provider, the sustainer and one who brings maturity is called Rubb. Al Rubb is one of the attribute of *Allah* for *Allah* cares for all His creation.

(17)Al-Risalah اَلرِّسَالَةُ

The office of prophetship is called Risalah. Rusul is the messenger or envoy of *Allah*. As *Allah* has provided for the development and growth of the universe,for human beings He has provided something more. Man has been created by *Allah* as free agent.He requires guidance to enable him to act (according to the guidance) in his own way. *Allah* has provided mankind with all necessary guidance for its perennial and universal needs. Risalah is an eloquent expression of *Allah's* love and concern for mankind. The guidance has been handed over to the prophets who communicated it to their fellow beings not only in words but in action i.e. by their example. Q33:21 "In the Messenger of Allah you have got a good example". Risalah implies that man is reformable and in him there is inherent good. The purpose of Risalah is to remind (Al-Zikr) what man already knows or can know. The purpose is to teach him what he does not or cannot know by himself. Risalah is to help man to find the Right Path[33] of *Allah*.

According to the *Quran* the messengers of *Allah* have played a role throughout history in communicating the message of *Allah* and demonstrating the way of life a man is supposed to follow.

The reason it was necessary to send Rusul at different times and to different people was to bring human beings back to the Right Path when they strayed.

All the Rusul (only 28 have been mentioned in the *Quran*) were chosen by *Allah* and were given one and the same message. The source of Risalah is *Allah*. The purpose of Risalah is to acquaint man with *Allah* and his Divine teachings, to establish truth and goodness, and to help man to realize the true purpose of his own creation and existence. The purpose is to help man to lead his life in a purposeful way. The teachings, of all the Rasul are identical constant and complementary. The Muslims believe in all the Rasuls and make no distinction between them

The term Rusul is also used for angels who bring Allah's message.

The Risalah came to a close with prophet Muhammad. With him the Din(15) of Islam(20) was completed.

The apostles or messengers were sent by Allah from among the human beings to deliver or to diseminate His message either to one race alone or to the entire mankind as in the case of the last messenger.

The Risalah of Muhammad was in response to the fervent prayer of Ibrahim Q2:129,151 and in fulfilment of the prophecy of Isa (Jesus).

The duties of the Risalah or the mission of the prophet as prescribed by Allah in the Quran are:

a) To recite to the believers the revelations of Allah and purifying them.

b) To teach them the scripture and wisdom as earlier they were in flagrant (manifest) error (darkness)[55].

c) To convey (to the believers) that those who do good work will be brought forth from darkness to light and that Allah has made good provision for them[8]

d) To warn that if the law of Allah is not followed the consequences will be untoward and adverse[9].

(18)Al Zakat اَلزَّكٰوةُ

Al-Zakat is the third duty enjoined to a Muslim. There is no equivalent in any other language or the vocabulary of any other religion to the *Quranic* term Al-Zakat. It is not just a form of charity or almsgiving . Charity and almsgiving are different and distinct from Al-Zakat. It is not simply an act of kindness. It is not merely a tax. Al-Zakat is a combination of all these and much more. It is a duty enjoined by *Allah* along with Salat(25) As-Sum(26) and Al-Hajj(8). It is to be under taken by Muslims in the interest of society as a whole.

There is an injunction in the *Quran*, (Q51:19) "In their wealth there was a right for the beggar and the person who did not ask" Al Zakat is the practical application of that injunction.

The literal and simple meaning of Zakat is purification. The technical meaning of the term Zakat, designates the annual amount in cash or kind which is to be paid by every well to do muslim.

Zakat not only purifies the property of the contributor but also purifies his heart. It purifies the heart of the recipient from envy and jealousy, from hatred and uneasiness.It fosters in his heart, instead, good will and warm wishes for the contributor. The recipient will not be under any obligation of the contributor as he will be if he receives alms or charity. The society at large will be purified and will free itself from class warfare and ill feelings between different classes.

Zakat is a most comforting consolation to the less fortunate people.

Tazkia means purifying the self as well as purying the remaining wealth by giving Zakat.

(19)Al- Tasbih التسبيح

Honoring *Allah* and precluding Him from all that is ascribed to Him is called Tasbih.Subhan *Allah* means praise of *Allah*. Subhan means pure and chaste but it implies pure from what is ascribed to Him. The testimony of Tauhid [57] implies that we must confirm all of *Allah*'s attributes which are stated in the *Quran*. This should be done without twisting the meaning or giving resemblance to anything created.

Attributes of *Allah* are important. They are very different from what a mortal brain can conceive. The attributes should be befitting His exalted position. Man in his ignorance uses derogative term such as the Christian believe that Jesus is the son of God or the belief of the idol worshippers of the pre-Islámic era that the idols are the daughters of *Allah*. *Allah* is untainted of what they say. He is above all that can be conceived. He is beyond all that can be ascribed to Him. A Muslim should repudiate any idea or suggestion that there can be any compeer of *Allah*. He is alive but His life is not only self sustaining but also sustains the entire universe. His life is eternal (not limiting to time and space) and non depending on other beings. His life and activity is perfect. He is greater than what can be conceived or expressed. It is in this sense that Subhan means pure and chaste and Subhan *Allah* thus means holiness and glorification to *Allah*.

Allah has bestowed the power of speech to human beings alone. It is therefore, incumbent on them to express the praise of Allah by their tongue in addition to performing other duties, (Q23:91) means *Allah* is beyond (free from) what they describe.

Subhan has a different connotation also. It means to do one's duty with full capacity (Q13:13) means the Thunder performs (its part) by His behest and the Angels (also) for fear of Him.

(20)Al Islam اَلْإِسْلَامُ

Islam means Commitment or confirmity to the will of *Allah*. Obedience and agreement to the divine law is Islam. This law is responsible to develop the inherent and latent capacities of everything in the universe to the point of its ultimate perfection. Every thing in the universe is a part of the grand design and is actively taking part in the all round evolution. The entire creation is proceeding on this way which is the Siratul Mustaqim [33]. Human society, because of the free will of man, is an exception to this universal law. Man according to the divine plan has to play his role deliberately and voluntarily. To perform his function properly he requires divine guidance. This is provided through Al-Risalah (17) Following the divine and universal law according to the life provided by the messenger of *Allah* is Islam. Thus Islam is the natural and most obvious path that is available to man.

The root SLM gives us As-Salam meaning peace as an Islamic way of greeting.

The Muslim is one who has surrendered or comitted himself to *Allah* or one who lives at peace.

"For Islam the word commitment is more positive active and responsible than are surrender or submission which the Orientalists and missionaries use".[1]

(21)Al-Mutashabih المتشابه

Al- Mutashibih means figurative. In the *Quran* there are two sets of Ayat: Ayat Muhkamat(12) and Ayat Mutashabihat. Ayat Muhkamat are the essence of the *Quran*. The other portion of the Book is called by the *Quran* itself Al-Mutashabihat which means allegorical, metaphorical and figurative. These ayaat have been made a source of dispute by man. Hence in the same ayaat in which these two terms Muhkamat and Mutashabihat have been used, it is made clear that those who are inclined to cause mischief and crave for discord are always after them to give them their own interpretations;although according to the *Quran* none knows about the relationship of the Mutashabihat except *Allah*.Those who are of sound knowledge(Rasikhoona-fil Ilm) only could say, "We believe therein the whole is from our Lord." But it is only the men of understanding "Ulul Albab"who really pay heed(to the basic truth).

(22)Al- Shariat الشريعة

Islamic law based on the *Quran* and Hadith i.e. the sayings of the Prophet is called Shar'. Al-Shariat is the system incorporating the Islamic law.

----

1. Prof. T.B. Irving: Introduction to the Translation of the Quran.

The distinction between Al-Din(15) and Al-Shariat should be clear. The common teachings of all the prophets is Din. The detailed code of conduct or the canons comprising ways and modes of worship, standards of morals and life,laws that prescribe and judge between right and wrong are Al-Shariat. These details have been undergoing amendments from time to time and though each prophet had the same Din, he brought with him his Shariat that would suit the conditions of his own people and his own time. This served the purpose of training different people over all ages for a better civilization and equipping them with better morals. Din has not undergone any change. After the advent of Muhammad all the previous Shariats stand superceded.

The two major sources of Al-Shariat of Muhammad are the *Quran* and the Hadith.

Four great scholars Imam Abu Hanifa (699-767), Imam Malik (714-798), Imam Shafii (767-854) and Imam Ahmed bin Hanbal (780-955) have codified Al-Shariat. In spite of minor differences all the four schools are authentic. One can follow any of them in one's life.

(23) Al-Sheerk اَلشِّرْكُ

To worship others along with *Allah* is called Sheerk. Sheerk means polytheism, idolatory, paganism and it is opposite of Tauhid [57] Mushrik is such an associate r.

The polytheists have associated with *Allah* other beings that have:

a. Material existence such as fire, animals, stars,eminent personalities etc.

b. Those which are not perceptible. These are believed to be administering various functions in the universe.

According to Islam to worship both the above mentioned beings and to solicit their help is degrading for man.

(24)Al-Shifaat الشَّفَاعَة

Recommendation and intercession for forgiveness is called shifaat.

There are three types of Ayat, covering the procedure which *Allah* has prescribed for Shifaat.

a. No intercession will be accepted on the Day of Judgement (Q2:48).

b. There will be no intercession by any one except to whom *Allah* has given permission (Q20:109).

c. None will have power of intersession except him who has made covenant with *Allah* (Q53:26).

It is evident from the above ayaat that on the day of resurrection (judgement)*Allah* will himself give permission to the prophet Muhammed for intercession which necessarily be confirmed only to the extent of believers as in other ayaat the prophet is prohibited from praying for the forgiveness of the unbelievers,the polytheists and the hypocrites who died before repentance.The *Quran* is silent about how this privilege of intercession given to the prophet by *Allah* will be excercised on the Day of judgement, though there are many Ahadith in this regard. A reasonable conclusion should be that the prophet might intercede in the case of those believers who had committed sins but will not pray for a reward for such believers who do not have any righteous deeds to their credit because intercession excercised in this manner will not be beseeming for a prophet.It goes against justice(28).

(25)Al-Salat اَلصَّلٰوة

Salat is one of the most important practices of Islam. It is the second pillar of Islam. It is not only the daily worship, formal and ritualistic prayer (as different from spontaneous prayer) but forms the basic unit of organisation of Islamic society. It is incumbent on every Muslim to establish Salat which means connection or contact. The Salat can therefore be explained as contact prayer. It is a unique prayer in which there is contact of every individual with the Almighty and at the same time there is contact of every individual with the congregation.

The term Salat is also rooted in the word meaning to follow. Mussali as a derivative of the term means the person who prefers the Salat.

Salat as a term means to follow *Allah*. In this sense Salat and Rububiah(16) are akin to one other. *Allah* has provided a self operative system for the Rububiah of the universe. Man is the only disorderly element in nature. For the Rububiah of the human society Salat is a system which represents Rububiah.

The term Salat is also rooted in the word meaning to give movements to hips. The practice which creates movement and activity in the society is therefore, called Salat.

The term Salat if from *Allah* means blessing and if from man means prayer. Congregational prayer or worship is the obligatory or Fard prayers which have to be offered five fixed times a day. These prayers form the main component of the Salat. Salat should be performed with perfect devotion and concentrated attention. It should be performed with calm and modest piety.

Mussalla is a small mat, prayer rug or carpet. The word is also used for the praying place.

(26)Al-Saum اَلصَّوم

Al-Saum or fasting is the fourth pillar of Islam. To abstain from eating, drinking and carnal desires from dawn (about 1 1/2 hour before sun rise) to dusk (sun set) during the month of Ramadan,the ninth month of the Muslim calendar, in a prescribed manner is called Saum. Muslims observe Saum with the intention of complying with the order of *Allah*. They get puritiy and spiritual benefits as a reward. Some people have a wrong notion that abstaining from food for spells may be harmful. Far from weakening the body, Saum rejuvenates and invigorates it. Those who observe Saum as a Discipline do get the material benefits inherent in it.

Normally the Saum should not affect the daily avocations and it should not be a pretext for neglecting daily duties. Islam never approves -- much less demands of keeping vigil during the whole night and preserving the day in sleep and indolence"1

At the end of the fasting month, there is the grand festival, Idul Fitr, on the first day of the month of Shawwal which the Muslims celebrate with gaiety.

----

(27)Al-Ibadah اَلْعِبَادَة

Islamic worship giving reverence to *Allah* who is Mabood (object of worship) and who alone deserves all reverence is called Ibadat. Worship is an act giving reverence to the divine or superior being.

Ibadat is derived from Abd (slave) and it means submission. It portrays that *Allah* is our Master and we are His slaves. Our duty towards *Allah* is Ibadat. Islamic concept of Ibadat is very wide. If we guard our speech from falsehood, abuse and malice it constitutes Ibadat. If we follow the laws of *Allah* in our business dealings and daily life it is Ibadat.If we help fellow beings it is Ibadat.If we remove thorns and other obstacles from the road it is Ibadat. If, in broader sense, we remove hurdles from the greater path of humanity it is Ibadat.

In short all activities resulting from total commitment to the will of *Allah* and moulding one's life into the pattern of Islam are Ibadat. To help achieve this aim a set of formal Ibadat has been prescribed and made obligatory. It is called Salat(25) Salat serves as a course of training. The more assiduously we follow the training the better equipped we will be for bringing harmony between our ideals and practices.

1. Dr.Muhammed Hamidullah-Why Fast? Makka Masjid, Philadelphia.

(28)Al-Adl اَلْعَدْل

The term Al- Adl is used in the *Quran* both in the sense of justice and also in the sense of compensation, return, alternative or substitute.

This term is mostly used in the sense of justice as a synonym of the Arabic word qist.

There are two kinds of attributes which are associated with *Allah, one relates exclusively to His Being (Zat) and the other attributes are such which Allah* Himself desires to see them in His bondsmen. For example those Muslims who had adopted "the manners of *Allah*" have been directed by Him to declare that they have adopted the color of *Allah*. One of the outstanding aspect of *Allahs color is justice or Adl. Hence He is never un-just to His creatures. As against the attributes of Allah* which *Allah* desires man to adopt, the other attributes which are exclusive to His Being are not to be shared by His creatures. To make others join Him in these attributes is Sheerk(23) which the *Quran* so forcefully denounces.

Salvation of man will depend on the day of Judgement not only on grounds of justice but also on the basis of *Allah's* Mercy. Hence He declares in the *Quran* that He has made the excersise of mercy incumbent on Himself.

As it has already been mentioned above a believer has to be just in his dealings with his fellow beings as *Allah* is with His creatures. Hence several injunctions have been issued in the *Quran* for the believers. One is directed to the prophet himself "Unto this then summon (them O Muhammad) and be you upright as you are commanded and follow not their lusts but say I believe in whatever revelation *Allah* has sent down, and I am commanded to be just....."42:15

(29)Al-Aaqibah اَلْعَاقِبَة

Al-Aqibah means end, consequence, sequel, outcome, final issue of all things, destiny of all things, or result. None of these words, however, give the exact and total meaning of the term Al-Aqibah.

Allah has by His own will established laws of life, the main being the law of cause and effect. According to this law man has to reap both in this world and in the other what he has sown with his own hands. If one takes to the straight path [33] in this world he is bound to reach the right destination. If one goes astray and takes to crooked ways of living he is bound to get in recompense[13] evil, grief, and pain as his due. According to the Quran one will earn only that for which he strives. Q2:286. Evil will be the result of evil action. Al-Aqibat, end or result (whether immediate or eventual) of an evil action will be nothing but evil, and one cannot expect good as an outcome of an evil action like Kufr(35) fisq(32) or transgression i.e. exceeding the bounds prescribed by Allah. When the Quran says that the Sunnat Allah does not change, it means that immutable are the laws of life, laid down by Allah himself by His own will. This truth applies both to the present and future life of man as it was applicable to him in the past. Q3:137. The Quran gives discretion to man to take to whatever way of living he likes after showing him the Din Al-Islam as the right way of living. Similarly it gives freedom of action also with a warning that the disbelievers will come to know that the happy sequel (aqibat) will be the lot of the believers alone and the wrong doers will never get falah[45] or success Q6:135.

(30)Al-Fard الفرض

Al-Fard means that which is obligatory. It is used for those rules and ordinances of Islam which are said to have been established and enjoined by *Allah* Himself as distinguished from those which are established upon the precept or practice of the prophet and which are called Sunnah.

(31)Al-Fujur الفجور

Al- Fujur means wrong, wickedness or lewdness. When man was created and his soul was fashioned and perfected, it was inspired by Allah with the sense of good and evil. It is left to man either to keep up its purity if he seeks to have falah [45] or to suppress it (soul) to stunt its growth and meet with inevitable failure. The Quran then shows man how to strife for his self purification or enlighenment of his soul. Invariably it refers to righteous action like giving of alms as a means of obtaining purification of the soul. Q92:18.

(32)Al-Fisq اَلْفِسْقُ

Al-Fisq means to act against the agreement. As a term Al-Fisq means the breaking of the covenant with *Allah* i.e. the following or disregarding the injunctions after accepting Islam.

Fasiq is a person who knows *Allah* but performs none of His commands. Fasiq is a reprobate person, neglectful and careless in his behaviour. Evidence of a Fasiq is not admissable in Islamic Courts. He is not regarded as a Muslim citizen although he may profess Islam.

Quran used the term Fasiq for human beings. In pre Islamic period this word was not used for human beings in this sense.

(33)Al-Qalb اَلْقَلْب

Al- Qalb means that which turns to one side and the other.The synonym of Qalb used in the Quran is fuad. The literary meaning of Qalb is heart. It is specified in the Quran that the place of heart is in the breast. Hence to translate qalb as mind is not correct.

When the Quran refers to qalb it is actually not referring to the out ward or the physical function of the heart but to its inward capacities. While utilising the potentialities or the capacities of the heart in the light of the Quranic guidance the personality of momin is built up. In other words Qalb represents the inner self of man, which has inclinations, tendencies, feelings Q6:43 or emotions Q53:11. According to the Quran, qalb is depicted as a seat of doubts Q9:45 and as the abode of faith Q5:41 and Q49:7. It is also shown as a bed of pollution Q9:77 and disease Q2:10 and rust Q3:14 Then the Quran points out its specific capacities like soundness Q37:84, contentment Q 16:106 satisfaction Q13:28 and Q48:4, anguish Q3:156, remorse Q50:33 and power to respond either to guidance Q64:11 or to misguidan ce Q61:5. The Quran also reveals that the heart is the abode of compassion and mercy.

Thus according to the Quran, the inner personality of a true momin (which is always reflected in his actions) is a combination of sound heart, enlightened mind and a pure soul. It is this inner personality which is totally at peace with the will of Allah and it is called in the Quran as nafs-e-mutmaina[51]

(34)Al-Qiyamah اَلْقِيٰمَةُ

Al-Qiyamah literally means standing up. In the *Quran* it means the Day of Resurrection.

The arising (of men at the resurrection) and at Sa'a, the Hour (or Day of Judgement) come under the general term Al-Ma'd "the returning" i.e. the return of life after death.

The phrase Yawmul- Qiyamah occurs 70 times in the *Quran*.

(35)Al-Kufr اَلْكُفْرُ

Al Kufr means disbelief, infidelity, blasphemy or ingrati tude. It is also the refusal and active opposition to anything that the prophet of Islam preached. The word Kafir is applicable only when the message is conveyed and if it is opposed.

Kafir is a disbeliever or an infidel. Kafir is one who covers or hides truth.

Kuffar or Kafiroon are both plural of Kafir.

Kufr implies a deliberate rejection of Faith as opposed to a mistaken idea of *Allah* or Iman(3) which is not inconsistent with an earnest desire to see the truth.

(36)Al-Malaikah اَلْمَلٰٓئِكَةُ

Belief in the existence of beings called angels is common to various faiths. It is also a fundamental belief of Islam. According to the *Quran* men are not the only beings created by *Allah*. Another order of beings are angels who act as *Allah's* agents and serve Him in many a way. They have not been endowed with free will. According to the *Quran* Malaik are absolutely obedient to *Allah* and they are commissioned with various functions in the universe. They meticulously perform the duties assigned to them by *Allah*. This is their worship and they are engaged in their worship and service to Him. The Angels have been assigned various duties: to administer *Allah's* punishments,to convey His messages and to perform various other functions such as Michael administering rain Raad causing thunder, etc.

Allah conveyed His revelations to the prophets including Muhammad, through Jibril (Gabriel), Jibril is also mentioned in the *Quran* as Rooh-ul Ameen, Ar- Rooh, RoohulQuds.

The belief in Al-Malaikah is complementary to monotheism. By accepting Al- Malaikah as a part of *Allah's* creation, obediently serving *Allah* this belief extricates the conceptof Tawheed[57] from all probable impurities and makes it free from the danger of Sheerk.(23)

(37) Al-Taqwa — اَلتَّقْوٰی

Taqwa means heedfulness, to be cautious and to save. As a term Al-Taqwa means to abstain from sin and from the consequences of sin. It means to restrain or guard one's behavior from evil. It implies righteousness piety and good conduct. Taqwa influences the activities, behaviour, manner and character of a Muslim. Taqwa is the quality of heeding (*Allah's* decree) or heedfulness. The *Quran* never tires of playing upon the terms by repetition, expansion, variation or clarification. The term Taqwa with its derivatives has been mentioned in the *Quran* about 250 times. The *Quranic* term like the others, has received different treatment from various translators. Everyone is partly true.

Taqwa requires a proper attitude of the mind by grasping the presence of *Allah*, the nature and limitations of human life. Taqwa requires judicious use of wealth, proper use of physical, mental, moral and spiritual abilities and faculties of man. It demands a high degree of self control over one's emotions like anger, greed, vanity etc. A moral capacity for forgiveness, patience, piety, righteousness and meaningful faith are inter related and all pour into one channel. They lead to Islam and build up a true Muslim.

"Taqwa is a particular attitude of man towards cosmic social phenomena not excluded. It has been metaphorically described as the care and attention of a person who passes along a narrow track both side bordered with thorny bushes. If this state of human activity with regard to the selection of right way for a right cause is based in the fear of *Allah* then it will be known as Taqwa"1

Muttaqi means God fearing and pious person. Muttaqin (plural of Muttaqi) are the heedful, those who do their duty to religion cautiously.

----

1. Dr. M. Riaz Kirmani's paper: *Quranic* Method of Enquiry in "Quest For New Science".

EXPLANATORY NOTES ON THE REPRESENTATIVE WORDS OF THE *QURAN*.

[1]. [Al-Adhan] اَلأَذَانُ

Literally Al-Adhan means anouncement. In Islam the call or the summons to congregational prayers is called Al-Adhan. The Muadhin is one who loudly proclaims or pronounces, Al-Adhan calling the believers to come to perform the Salat (25).

The English rendering of Al-Adhan is:

Allah is most Great.	*Four times*
I testify that there is no god but *Allah*.	*Twice*
I testify that Muhammad is the Messenger of *Allah*.	*Twice*
Come to As-Salat.	*Twice*
Come to Success.	*Twice*
Allah is most Great.	*Twice*
There is no god but *Allah*.	*Once*

In Al-Adhah for the early morning (Fajr) Salat after the words come to success (Falah) is added "Salat is better than sleep" twice.

[2]. Al-Imamah اَلإِمَامَةُ

The primary sense of the word Imam is that of being foremost;hence it may mean:

A. Leader of Al-Ummah [3]
B. Leader in congregational prayer.
C. Model, pattern or example.
D. A book of guidance and instruction. Q11:17
E. A book of evidence or record. Q36:12

[3]. Al-Ummah اَلْاُمَّةُ

Al-Ummah literally means a people, company, group, a nation or a sect. The word occurs about forty times in the *Quran* and it applies to the followers of the prophets viz. Ummatu Ibrahim meaning the followers of Ibrahim, Ummatu Muhammad meaning the followers of Muhammad etc.

Muhammad's (PBUH) Ummat is a band of people - the comrades or companions of the Prophet (PBUH) and those who followed in their footsteps with a mind moulded by the *Quran*. It is to this band the *Quran* addresses the appelation *Ummatan Wasata, a community living a balanced life and "serving as a pattern unto others, even as the prophet has been a pattern unto you (Q2:143). It was this Ummatan Wasata* which the Prophet of Islam organized into a state, an organization which was intended to serve as a nucleus of a world order.

[4]. Al-Amr Bil-Maruf اَلْاَمْرُ بِالْمَعْرُوْفِ

This word is a combination of two words Amr and Maruf. The word Amr is comprehensive and includes:

A. An order,that which is enjoined or a command.
B. A purpose, design or will. Q18:82
C. Working, doing, carrying out or execution of a design, affairs. Q79:5 In many cases some of these meanings run together.

Maruf means whatever is prevalent, whatever is in usage, or in common practice (of decency), whatever is recognised (as just and right). Amr Bil Maruf is imperative meaning adopt whatever is prevalent or current in the society (to the extent it is not objectionable.) One fundamental policy of Islam should be kept in mind: Islam is a natural religion. It is not imposed or implanted on the society. Practices, morality even the modes of worship which are found by the Rusul(17) in common practice are enjoined on their respective Ummah[3] as part of the one Din, the original one. Necessary modifications are made to suit the basic principles of Din(15) and such practices which from time to time creep in and are not in conformity with Islam are eliminated. Thus we see that Salat, Sawm and Hajj were in vogue at the advent of Islam. They were continued with slight modifications and improvements. The custom of Pagan Arabs to praise their forefathers at the conclusion of Hajj, was considered as innovation in the original Hajj as prescribed by Ibrahim and was discontinued.

[5]. Ahlul Bait or Aalul Bait أَهْلُ الْبَيْتِ

Ahl-ul Bait or Al-ul Bait literally means people of household. In the *Quran* it is referred to the wife of Ibrahim Q11:73, people of the household Q28:12 and to the wives of Muhammed (PBUH) Q33:33. The code of conduct prescribed therein was extended to other members of the family of Muhammad (PBUH).

[6]. Al-Ayah اَلْاٰيَةُ

Al-Ayah means a sign portent, token or miracle. With reference to the *Quran* it applies to the smaller portions or sentences of the *Quran* which are generally but wrongly called the verses. For Allah communicates with men through verbal signs, revelation or wahi[61] and through natural signs. Allah continuously reveals His messages through natural phenomenon which are signs (ayat) of different aspects of His nature in the physical universe, His law is expressed through different phenomenon such as the objects of nature. His law is also expressed through compassion, justice, power etc. These natural ayat are directly available for all men without any intermediary. For more information se paragraph 2 of the preface and also [61].

[7]. Al-Bidah اَلْبِدْعَة

All innovations which alter the original concept of Islam in doctrine or practice is Bidah. In other words innovation in matters of Din(15) are Al-Bidat. With the intention of earning Thawab(6) if some act is performed for which there is no authority, then that act will be regarded as Al-Bidah. Every novelty or innovation is not Al-Bidah.

[8] and [9]. Al-Basharah Wal Nazarah

اَلبشَارَةَ وَالنَّذَارَةُ

Al-Quran is an authoritative proclamation consisting of adominations and promises. Al-Basharat means good tidings and promises. Al-Bashir means one who brings good tidings. In the quran Al-Basharat is a part of the prophetic mission ie Risalah(17). As a part of the prophetic mission, the Rasul is enjoined to convey (to the believers) the good tidings, that those who do good work (Amal-Salih) will get good reward from *Allah*. In the *Quran* Al-Bashir has been used for Muhammed Q2:119.

Al-Nazarah means adomination warning or caution. One who warns is called Al-Nazeer.

Al-Nazarah is a part of the prophetic mission. The *Quran* enjoins in the prophet to warn the people that if the law of ***Allah*** is disregarded the consequences will be disastrous. In the ***Quran*** prophet Muhammed (PBUH) is addressed as Al-Nazir Q34:28.

[10]. Al-Balagh

اَلْبَلٰغُ

Al-Balagh means that which is propagated, transmitted, disseminated, delivered, spread or communicated. In the Quran it also applies to the message that is transmitted or delivered by the prophet Q14:52. Other derivatives related to this word which are used in the Quran are Balaghah meaning to reach,ablagha, meaning to deliver, diseminate or propagate Q7:79. Balagha means that which has reached maturity Q6:149.

Tabligh means to propagate, transmit, disseminate, deliver, spread, or communicate the message of Allah. Tabligh is obligatory to every Muslim.

One of the main purposes of tabligh is to convey the message of the Quran to others with the intention of invitation. In addition to this basic duty it is the privilege of every Mumin to invite others to goodness, to enjoin the right (which is universally acceptable to one and all[4]) and to forbid the wrong (which is repulsive to human conscience itself [56]). It is also his privilege to enjoin kindness and piety along with exhorting others to patience and forbearance ie sabr [31].

It is the common privilege of every practicing Muslim to undertake the task of tabligh, to let the religion or din of Allah triumph over all other cults which others have wrongly taken to as their religion.

[11]. Al-Ittiba الاتباع

Literal meaning of Al-Iteba is to follow or to pursue as is evident from its usage in Q2:102, 2:120 or 3:30. It also means seeking as in Q5:16. This word is commonly used in the sense of following the straight path and the path of the prophets or of Allah. It is also used in the sense of following an approved custom Q2:178.

[12]. Al-Tawbah التوبة

Al-Tawbah literally means one who turns (pays attention) Hence one of the attributes of *Allah* is the Relenting (At-Tawwab). With refrence to man Tawba means repentance with refrence to *Allah* it means 'to relent'.

In the *Quran* Al-Tawbah is used for repentance. For repentance three ingredients are required: (a) the sinner must admit and acknowledge his or her wrong; (b) he or she must give it up and (c)he or she must resolve to aschew it for the future. Human nature is weak and one may have to return again and again for mercy. So long as he or she does it sincerely, *Allah* is oft Returning and the Most Merciful. For His Grace helps out the sinner's shortcomings.

Sincere and true repentance is called in the *Quran* as Tawbatan-Nusuh.

[13]. Al-Jaza الجزاء

Al-Jaza means reward, requital or recompense. According to the law of *Allah* there is full accountability for every action of the individual or of the community. If the action is good the result or reward will be good. If the action is bad it will end in disaster. Jaza therefore, applies to reward for good actions as well as to suffering for the bad actions. Al-Akhirat(1) is a continuation of this life. The life of compensation for good or bad deeds committed during the life on earth will be governed in this life as well as the life of hereafter.

[14] and [15]. Al-Jannah Wal Nar الجنة والنار

Al-Jannat means a garden. In the *Quran* it is referred to the regions of celestial bliss or the paradise. Plural of Al-Jannah is Al-Jannat.

Al-Nar literally means "the fire". The word occurs in the *Quran* very frequently for the hell viz.Q2:22 "Fear the fire whose fuel is men and stones" Some scholars understand the reference to fire as figurative.

[16]. Al-Hadith الحديث

The literal meaning of Al-hadith is narration Q99:4, report Q39:23, discourse Q93:11, tale, legend Q34:19,51,56.

When hadith is used as a verb it means to cause, to arouse, to kindle, to develop Q2:113.

It is to be noted that this word hadith is not used in the *Quran* just in the sense of reporting a matter or narrating an event or to talk about something but the use of the word implies that the narration is always with a purpose, the purpose being to let it serve as a reminder. Hence we find in one or two ayah, the use of the word hadees along with the word Zikr Q18:70,20:113.

In the post Quranic literature hadith in relation to prophet Muhammad (PBUH) is used to cover not only his sayings but also his actions. This seems to be justifiable to we Muslims on the ground that there was no difference between his words and actions, as he did what he said and said what he did. In short there was uniformity in his words and deeds.

We are finding nowadays an insignificant trend both at lower level and a higher among the Muslim intelligentia to consider hadith as redundant, when the Quran by itself is "fairest hadith and Tafsir" Q39:23 and 25:33. But the Quran does not lend any support to such line of thinking when it determines the mission of the prophet himself Q2:151. The *Quran* entrusts the Prophet (PBUH) the task of explaining to mankind that which has been revealed for them so that they reflect Q16:44. Thus in the light of the Quran, the correct view should be that hadith (tradition of the Prophet PBUH) is the fairest companion of the *Quran*. As hadith is the word of Allah (explained and put into practice by the prophet) to shirk hadees is to miss the full understanding of the Quran and its blessings. It is for we muslims particularly the scholars to cull out from the hadith literature the valuable treasure in which the Prophet (PBUH) has explained the Quran to others.

[17]. Al-Hisab اَلْحِسَابِ

Al-Hisab means the account. When used with the Yawm ie Yawm-Al Hisab it means the Day of reckoning or the Day of account. It refers to the Day of judgement. The concept demonstrates the fact of accountability which Islam strongly stresses as necessary for a responsible person.

[18]. Al-Hashr اَلْحَشْرِ

Al- Hashr literally means going forth from one place and assembling in another. The word is used in the *Quran* in two different connotations: (a) an emigration vide Q59:2 "It was He who drove forth from their homes those people of the Book ie the Jews who misbelieved at the first emigration. and (2) an assembly vide Q27:17" His hosts of the jinn and men and birds were assembled for Solomon.

The term Yawmul-Hashr is used for the Day of judgement or the Day of Resurrection ie the day when the dead shall come up from their graves and assemble for judgement Q50:42 "We cause to live, and We cause to die. To Us shall all return. On the Day when the earth shall swiftly cleave assunder over the dead,this gathering will be easy to Us".

[19] and [20]. Al-Haqq wal Batil الحق والباطل

Al-Haqq means right. Right has many shades of meaning:

A. Right in the sense of having a right to something.
B. Right in the sense of straight conduct as opposed to wrong.
C. Justice.

Haqq is used in the *Quran* for that which is true ie the word of *Allah, or the Way of Allah*.

Al-Batil as opposed to Al- Haqq means false. In the *Quran* Al-Batil applies to false in doctrine.

[21]. Al-Hikmah الحكمة

Al-Hikmah literally means "the wisdom" In the *Quran* Al-Hikmah is used to express a knowledge of the essence, attributes of *Allah* and results of things as they exist viz Q2:272. "He *(Allah) brings the wisdom (Al-Hikmah) unto whom He pleases" The Quran* is mentioned as Al-Hikmah in the *Quran*.

Hukum literally means judgement or decision. It also means wisdom, discretion, Knowledge and power to see things in their true perspective.

[22]. Al-Khilafah الخلافت

The office of the khalifah is called Al-Khilafat. Khalifah (plural khulafa) means "to leave behind". In English it is wrongly spelt as "caliph". Khalifah means a successor, a lieutenant, a vicegerent or a deputy.The word is used in the *Quran* for man as the vicegerent of *Allah* on earth.vide Q2:28 "When your Lord said to the angels 'I am about to place a vicegerent (khalifa) on the earth' they said Will you place therein one who will do mischief and blood-shed therein?"

Khulafa also means (a) people with power to mobilize all that is on earth Q27:62. (b) successors or inheritors who will inherit the earth and succeed one after another Q24:55.

In Islam khalifa is the title given to the successor of Muhammad. In this sense khalifa and Imam[2] and Ulu l-Amr[60] are all synonyms. Khalifa is vested with authority in all matters of state both civil and religious, as long as he rules in conformity with the law of the *Quran* and Hadith.

It is held to be an essential principle in the establishment of the office, that there shall be only one khalifa at the same time; for the prophet said "when two khulafa have been set up, put the latter to death and preserve the earlier (chosen) for the latter is a rebel.

Khalifa occurs twice in the *Quran* where in refering to Dawud and Adam. It signifies one in authority or excercising authority. In its application to the basic meaning of the term Khalifa is successor.

[23] and [24]. Al-Khawareq wal Istedraj

الخَوارِق وَالاسْتدراج

Kharqu-l-Adah literally means the break with the natural course, or that which is contrary to the usual course of nature. This word is used for miracles: (a) Mujizah [38] is miracle worked by prophets (b) karamat wonders performed by Aulia (plural of wali [5]) (c) istidraj is wonder worked by the power of Shaitan.

[25]. Al- Dhikr اَلذِّكر

In the root DHKR it means to remember, to bear in mind, to recall, to cherish the memory of someone as a precious possession. In the causative form it means to remind, to reflect, bear in mind (for one's own benefit) In the *Quran* we are asked to solemnly remember in our own minds and to proclaim, praise and be grateful of *Allah's* favours on us (Q2:231).

The *Quran* is mentioned as Al-Dhikr in the *Quran*.

[26]. Al-Ruh اَلرُّوح

Al-Ruh means the spirit or the soul. In the *Quran* Al-Ruh means special angel (It is generally agreed that it refers to Jibriel). Ruh-ul Ameen (the faithful spirit) occurs in the *Quran* (26:193). It also applies to angel Jibriel. Similarly Ruh-Ul Qudus (the holy spirit) also applies to Jibriel.

In most post *Quranic* literature Ruh and Nafs[51] are used interchangeably and both are applied to human spirit and angels. Ruh also means breath of life. The *Quran* is mentioned as Ar-Ruh in the *Quran*.

[27]. Al-Sajdah اَلسَّجْدَة

Al- Sajdah literally means prostration. In the *Quran* Al-Sajdah means prostration before *Allah*. Al-Sajdah is an act of worship in which the person's fore-head touches the ground. As-Sajdah is the title of Sura 32, the 15th ayat of which says "They only believe in Our signs who, when they are reminded of them, fall down adoring and celebrate the praises of their Lord."

[28]. Al-Sunnah اَلسُّنَّة

Al- Sunnah literally means a path or way; a manner of life. In Islam it is used to express the custom or manner of life. The tradition which records either the sayings and doings of Prophet Muhammed (PBUH) are called Al-Sunnah.

Sunnah is the embodiment of the views and practices of the earliest Islamic community. It functions as most authoritative interpretation of the text of the *Quran*.

[29]. Al-Shaitan اَلشَّيْطٰن

The dictionary meaning of Al-Shaitan is very proud and rebellious one among Jin, men and animals.

In religious thought Shaitan is the power that opposes the Almighty in the hearts of men. He whispers his insideous suggestions in their ears and makes his proposals seductive to them. There is, however, no hint of dualism, for the Shaitan has no real power over man. He owes his success to craft alone. He cannot exploit that success for he is afraid of *Allah* and leaves men in the lurch as soon as he has persuaded them to sin.

Al-Shaitan is a regular Arabic form and it is borrowed from the Ethiopic language which in turn is derived from Hebrew.

In the *Quran* the word Shaitan has been used 68 times.

[30]. Al-Shahadah اَلشَّهَادَةُ

Shahadah means witness. Telling the truth before a judge has always been difficult as it is today because of the fear of the vested interests or because of various considerations. An upright and honest man without fear or favour will speak out the truth. In the *Quran* there are clear injunctions to come forward without hesitation and to give true evidence when called (Q65:2). There is also the injunction not to hide evidence (testimony). As in everyday life appearing as true and dignified witness in more important issues before the nations is also important. The *Quran* says that the Muslims have been made a justly balanced intermediary Ummah[3] to be witness over the nations (Q2:143) Greater is the importance of bearing witness to the fundamental principles for which one as a Muslim has to live, struggle and if necessary to die. The basic truth around which all other (truths) revolve is the existence of the Supreme Being. The first and the foremost duty and in fact the religious obligation of a Muslim is to be a Witness, if necessary against the entire humanity and declare Tawhid [57].

For the Muslims the first of the acts of worship is to believe with the heart and declare with the tongue that there is no diety except *Allah* and that Muhammad (PBUH) is the messenger of *Allah*. This is expressed in the testimony "Ashhuadan la ilaha il *Allah* wa Ashhuadana Muhammadan Rasul *Allah"(I bear witness that there is no deity except Allah* and I bear witness that Muhammad (PBUH) is the messenger of *Allah*.

[31]. Al- Sabr الصَّبْر

The Arabic word Sabr implies many shades of meaning, which it is impossible to comprehend in one English word. It implies, (a) patience in the sense of being thorough and not hasty. (b) patient perseverance, constancy, steadfastness, firmness of purpose, (c) systematic as opposed to spasmodic or erratic action (d) a cheerful attitude of resignation and understanding in sorrow, defeat or suffering as opposed to murmuring or complaining but saved from mere passivity or listlessness by the element of constancy or steadfastness.

The patient perseverance, Sabr and Salat (Q2:153) is not merely passivity. It is active striving in the way of *Allah*. Such striving is the spending of one's self either through our property or through our own lives or the lives of those near and dear to us.

[32]. Al-Sadaqah الصَّدَقَة

Al-Sadaqah is derived from Sidq meaning to be righteous or truthful. In the *Quran* it is used for almsgiving or charity vide Q2:265. Kind speech and pardon are better than almsgiving (Sadaqah) followed by annoyance, for *Allah* is rich and clement. Sadaqa as verb means to speak the truth. This points to the fact that the giving of alms by a Muslim is itself a witness to the truthfulness of his religion.

The word Sadaqah is used in two different senses. In the first place it is frequently employed as synonymous with Al- Zakat (18) that is the poor rate which is obligatory and of which the rate is fixed vide Q7:58.

The other use of the word is in the sense of voluntary almsgiving. Sadaqah is used in this sense in the remaining ayat of the *Quran* vide Q2:263 etc.

Sadiqin means men who persevere (in righteousness) Q33:35. Siddiqin means righteous Q4:69.

Sadiqin and Siddiqin are the band of people that the *Quran* aims to form by building up their minds in its own fashion to create a healthy society.

[33]. Al-Siratul-Mustaqim اَلصِّرَاطُ الْمُسْتَقِيْمُ

Sirat is one of the foreign based words in the Quran. Sirat from Latin strata means street, its English derived descendant. In the *Quran* Sirat occurs 38 times in all of which it is used for Sirat-Al-Mustaqim or the Right Way of religion.

In the *Quran* Islam is referred to as Sirat-Al-Mustaqim, "It is *Allah* who is my Lord then worship Him. This is the Staight Way" Q3:44.

The *Quran* is also mentioned as Sirat-Al-Mustaqim in the *Quran*.

[34] and [35]. Al-Islah Wal-Fasad اَلْاِصْلَاحُ وَالْفَسَادُ

The meaning of the word islah is reformation. It signifies behaviour that is righteous, just and dignified. In the Quran it refers to reformation both of one's own self Q 3: 89 and of others Q 26: 19. Those who act righteously ie. perform Amal-e-Salih Q2:62. are called Salihin and those who reform others are called Muslihin or Muslihun.

The reformation of the self is expressed by good deeds ie amal-e-saleh. Inthe Quranic usage Amal Salih means righteous in the action. It is often used in the Quran with iman (3) and both are regarded as condition for success in this world as well as in the hereafter. According to the Quran the characteristics of Salihin are that:

a) they believe in Allah and the last day (1)
b) enjoin right conduct [4] and forbid indecency [56]
c) vie with one another in good deeds Q3:114.

With reference to society the Quran uses the word Islah in the sense of restoration of order Q7:56, peace making, promotion of good will Q 2:182 and 4:114 or improvement of one's lot Q2:220.

The literal meaning of Al-fasad is misbelief, corruption, confusion and disorder.

In the *Quran* Fasad is used against the word Islah. It means creating confusion and exploiting weaker sections of society by following path other than the path of *Allah*.

According to the Quran Jihad (7) means striving in the way of Allah for extermination of Fasad from the earth and establishment of peace so that the religion of peace ie. Islam(20) prescribed by Allah for mankind is not disturbed. Hence terrorism which leads to worst kind of Fasad is something quite alien to Islam and against its very spirit. The Quran teaches an historical lesson that whenever the fire of war-fare was ignited by man it was extinguished by Allah so that cloisters in churches, synagogues and mosques may not be destroyed by the mischief of man. Allah as the author of peace, As-salam (20) and as grantor of security Al-Mumin (3) dislikes Fasad or disorder on the earth. A Muslim enters into a covenant with Allah to remove Fasad from the face of the earth by striving with his possessions and his life to get in return paradise. The Quran calls this a goodly transaction Q9:111.

[36]. Al-Taharah اَلطَّهَارَةُ

Al-Taharah means purification. Cleanliness is the basic requirement of Islam. According to Islam cleanliness is next to godliness. For performing Salat cleanliness of the dress, body and place is necessary. One has to make abulution (wudu) before Salat.

[37]. Al-Zulm اَلظُّلْمُ

Al-Zulm literally means not putting a thing in the proper place. Zulm implies harm, wrong, injustice or transgression and may have reference to one self; when wrong is done to others it implies tyranny and oppression; the idea of wrong naturally connects itself with darkness which is another shade of meaning carved with the root word.

In *Quranic* usage Zulm is of three kinds (a) between man and *Allah* (b) between man and man and (c) man towards his self i.e. Nafs[51].

[38]. Al-Mujizah المُعْجِزَة

Al-Mujizah lterally means the overwhelming or that which renders powerless. It now stands for miracle. The *Quran* denies miracles in connection with Muhammad (PBUH) whereas it emphasises that the *Quran* is peerless and matchless. It stresses on the merits of the signs i.e. Ayat [6] mistakenly called the verses of the *Quran*. Even in post *Quranic* literature the *Quran* is mentioned as the chief miracle of Muhammad (PBUH).

The term karamah is used in connection with the saints; it differs from Al-Mujizah in so far as it denotes nothing but a personal distinction granted by *Allah* to Awlia.

[39]. Al Adhab اَلْعَذَابُ

Opposite of Al-Falah[45] meaning failure, misery, punishment, divine wrath, penalty, agony, anguish, disturbed state of society and of mind of the individual.

Islam calls to all that is good; enjoins the right and forbids the wrong. If this call is not heeded the inevitable result will be Al-Adhab.

The divine judgement strike the individual as well as the entire nation. It is mainly the un-belief in the eternal truths, the opposition of the prophetic mission and rebellion against *Allah* that are condemned for eternal punishment.

[40]. Al-Amal اَلْعَمَلُ

The literal meaning of Al-Amal is act, action, work, and deed. This word is used in the *Quran* both for evil action Q5:90 and for good deed or righteous action Q9:120.

This word is commonly used in the *Quran* along with faith ie Iman(3) with equal emphasis on both. Just as faith without action is undesirable, so also good actions without faith are futile for a Muslim. The *Quran* lays great emphasis on good works along with right faith. In Christianity as expounded by St. Paul, no value has been attached to good works, nor are they felt to be necessary. Faith in Jesus is sufficient for Salvation. To reform this corruption in Christianity as preached by St. Paul, the *Quran* lays much emphasis on good works.

[41]. Al-Iste Adha الاِسْتِعَاذَه

The literal meaning of Al-Iste Adha is seeking refuge or protection in *Allah* against the evil powers particularly of the devil both from the jin and man Q7:200.

This word is also used for seeking protection of a source other than *Allah* Q72:6.

This word is used in a different form like Maadh-Allah to convey the meaning, may *Allah* forbid Q12:79.

[42]. Al-Maghfirah اَلْمَغْفِرَةُ

The word used in the *Quran* with a meaning similar to forgive, but each with a different shade of meaning are:

(a) Afa means to forget, to obliterate from one's mind.
(b) Safaha means to overlook, to turn away from, ignore, to treat a matter as if it did not affect one.
(c) Ghafara means to cover up something as *Allah* in His unlimited grace does to our sins. This word is particularly appropriate in *Allah's* attribute of Al-Ghaffar the One who forgives again and again. Human beings are imperfect. Committing a sin or making a mistake does not necessarilly deaden the human heart or stop moral growth. In fact man has enough sensibility to recognize his shortcomings. Man is capable of realizing to whom he should turn for guidance. *Allah* is ever prepared to respond to his sincere calls for help. *Allah's* forgiveness is Encompassing. Discrimination on the basis of sex, hereditary guilt or sin are alien to the spirit of Islam.

[43]. Al-Ghaib اَلْغَيْبُ

Al-Ghaib means the unknown the unseen. Iman-bil-Ghaib means faith in the unknown ie believing or having faith in what was previously unknown. In our day to day life we rely upon people who know in matters we do not know. Iman-bil-Ghaib signifies the achievement of knowledge of what was not known to us from one who knows. We do not know about *Allah* His attributes, His law (of rewarding for the good deeds and punishing for the bad deeds) His message, His Deen etc. The Rusul(17) possess all such knowledge. We recognise them by their sincerity and by the wisdom of the message and believe in what they say. This conviction is Iman-bil-Ghaib. Such truth-discerning attitude is essential for commitment to the way of *Allah*. We have no choice because there is no other medium than the Rasul for the true knowledge without which we cannot proceed rightly on the path of Islam.

[44]. Al-Fitnah اَلْفِتْنَةُ

Al-Fitnah means trial, test or temptation as in Q2:102. It also means tumult, sedition, oppression, persecution or suppression of some opinion by violence, force or threats as in Q2:217.

[45]. Al-Falah اَلْفَلَاحُ

Al-Falah means success, welfare, prosperity, freedom from anxiety and care. It is to be understood in a wide sense to include prosperity in our worldly affairs as well as in spiritual progress. In both cases it implies happiness and the attainment of our ambitions purified by the love of *Allah*.

In Al- Adhan [1] the believers are simultaneously called for Salat(20)and Falah. This only implies that Falah or welfare is the obvious result of Salat when it is established in the society.

The ideal Muslim community is happy, contended, untroubled by conflicts or stress, sure of itself, strong, united and prosperous.

Muflihin are those who have achieved the real success through the teachings of Islam. Muflihin are a band of people that the *Quran* aims to form by building up their minds in its own fashion to create a healthy society. Falah is different from Fauz, meaning achievement and accomplishment.

Opposite of Al-Falah is Al-Azab[39]

[46]. Al-Qadr اَلْقَدَرُ

Al- Qadr literally means measuring. The word is generally used for fate or predestination.

Taqdir is used in the Quran in three broad senses. Firstly, there is the field of what we may term the Divine initiative or of the operation of the laws of nature, Fitrat *Allah* or Sunnat *Allah*. They are signs of a plan of existence necessarilly conceived in advance or predetermined. Even human plans are pre determined, with the difference that man changes his plans as experience warrants him, whereas *Allah's* knowledge being perfect, His plan is never changed.

Secondly, there is the field of human initiative. Our own acts are mightier powers. The Quran has laid down definite injunctions. Man has to act in coformity with the laws of *Allah*

Lastly, there is the reaction on our life of the deeds of others. Sometimes they bring us joy and sometimes pain and suffering. Taqdir in this context expresses itself in one or two ways. It may be that those who have thus suffered had not in proper time anticipated the rise of evil tendencies in others. They did not exercise proper check on them or it may be that they knowingly abstained from interference. They have to pay for their failure to do so.

Much of our suffering at domestic, national or international level is preventable. If we allow evil to prosper it ammounts to criminal unconcern with what is going on around us. Not only the wrong doers are responsible for the suffering but also those who seemingly innocent, failed to prevent.

Taqdir in some form or the other is the name for the stage in which man has no say. This is the realm of Divine Veto. A stage does come when all that is humanly possible is done, and yet the result is not as humanly anticipated. Man has therefore to do his part and leave the result to *Allah*.

[47] and [48] Al-Furqan-wal Quran

اَلْفُرْقَانُ وَ اَلْقُرْاٰنُ

Furqan means judgment, or criterion. Discernment between right and wrong and standard by which we can judge between right and wrong is Furqan. The victory of Badr (towards the end of 2 H) was described in the *Quran* (Q8:41) as the day when the true was distinguished from the false. Al-Furqan is one of the names given to *Al-Quran*.

Al-*Quran* is the name of the holy Book revealed to prophet Muhammad from *Allah* during a period of 23 years through the angel Jibriel. The purpose of the *Quran* is "to evolve a mind which gives to the world its Salehin and Muttaqin(37) its Muqsitin and Muflihin[45] its Sadiqin[32] and Siddiqin[32] and rest of the order.... who live and work in full consciousness of *Allah* developed in them".1 Through the *Quran* only the soul of Islam can be understood. For more information see paragraph 2 of the Preface and also Al-Kitab[49].

----

1. Dr. Syed Abdul Lateef - The Mind Al-Quran Builds. Villa Academy, Aziz Bagh, Hyderabad, India.

[49]. Al-Kitab الكتاب

Al-Kitab means the Book. In Islam it refers to the Book of *Allah*. The third article of Iman(3) is to believe in the Books of *Allah* which He has sent down to mankind through His Rusul. There is a mention of some of the books viz. Book of Ibrahim, Taurat of Musa, Zaboor (Psalms) of Dawood, Injeel (Gospels) of Isa. Of the innumerable prophets sent by *Allah* in all ages and to all the people only 28 have been mentioned in the Quran. There is no mention of the names of the Books sent to the other prophets mentioned in the Quran or (to the prophets) not mentioned in the Quran. Therefore with regard to other existing religious books, we are not in a position to say with certainty whether they were originally revealed books or not. But we tacitly believe that whatever books have been sent down by *Allah* were all true.

> Of the books mentioned in the *Quran,* the books of Ibrahim are extinct and not traceable in the existing world literature. The other three Books are the Bible (The Old and the New Testament. The *Quran* informs us that people have changed and interpolated these books. *Allah's* works have been mixed up with texts of their own making. This corruption and pollution of the Books has been on such a large scale that even the Jews and the Christians themselves admit it. Moreover they do not possess the orginal Texts and have only the translation. We find that *Allah's* words and those of men have been mixed together in these books.

The Quran is the last of the divine Books sent by*Allah*. The text of the Quran is in tact and there is no change in it whatsoever. The Quran is the word of *Allah* and there is no mixture of words of any human being in it. In the Quran there is abundant evidence that it was revealed to Muhammad. The Quran is in the Arabic language which is a living language. The message of the Quran is not for one nation or one race but for the entire humanity.

Scripture is not a proper word for Al-Kitab.

[50]. Al- Mashiah اَلْمَشِيْئَةُ

The derivatives of the word Al-Mashiah have been used several times in the Quran though the word Al-Mashiah has not been used. It represents that which Allah wants or wills. Though it is the will of Allah or His intention (desire) Q4:26. that ultimately prevails,in the life of man in this world, yet He has of His own will given freedom of faith and action to man. In other words man is a creature with a will. It is left to him either to commit himself to the will of Allah and his pattern of life to the Divine pattern or to act according to his own desire against the will of *Allah*. In the former case he will be richly recompensed and in the latter case he will be retributed with disaster and grief.

It is man's good fortune that he is required to submit to the will of The Creator, who is just and merciful and does not want to harm any of His creatures

"The misfortune which befalls you is (the result of your own action) from yourself" says the *Quran* 4:79.

The Quran shows in detail for the guidance of man, how the will of Allah operates, both in governing the universe and the life of man on earth and how He fulfils the ways of Allah (sunnat Allah) the Quran demands man to submit to the will of Allah.

[51]. Al-Nafs اَلنَّفْسُ

In the *Quran* Nafs means soul Nafs and its plurals Anfus and Nufus have two uses in the *Quran* (a) self or person as in Q3:61 "Let us call, ourselves and yourselves". In six ayaat Nafs refers to *Allah* as in Q5:116 "Thou (*Allah*) does know what is in myself (Jesus) but I do not know what is in Thyself (Nafsika)" At one place it refers to gods ie Q25:3 "They (aliha) do not possess for themselves (anfusihim) any harm or benefit at all.

And (b) human soul as in Q6:93 while the angels stretch forth their hands (saying) send forth your souls (anfus).

Nafs-e-Mutmainnah (Q89:28) according to the *Quran* is the soul which is at perfect tranquility and it is the result of the inner personality of a true Mumin (which is always reflected in his good deeds).

[52]. Al-Munafiq اَلْمُنٰفِق

Al-Munafiq means the hypocrite. The type of these men is what is called Mr. Facing -both ways in John Bunyan's Pilgrim's Progress. Such men declare that they are always with the Right but calmly intrigue with Evil and injustice and even make Injustice their judge if their personal interests are served in that way. When Islam was not yet powerful the hypocrites pretended to be with the Muslims, but were in league with their enemies. When *Allah* granted victory to Islam their position became awkward.

[53]. Al-Hijrah اَلْهِجْرَة

Al-Hijrah means emigration. It does not mean flight but breach, dissolution of an association based on dissent, in the place of which a new connection is formed. Muhajirun means emigrants. The earliest Muhajira i.e., migrant was Hajira the wife of Prophet Ibrahim who migrated to the distant and forlorn city, Makkah with her son Ismail. It is most probable that she got her name Hajira because of the migration. The followers of Muhammed (PBUH) migrated to Abyssinia in the first instance. This word is applied in Islamic literature to those who migrated to Madina for the cause of Islam. The word Muhajir is not applied to the Prophet himself but to those who migrated with him, before him or after him and later made up a considerable portion of the population of Madina. The followers of the Prophet who were natives of Madina were given the name Ansar to distinguish them from the Muhajirun because the immigrants were mainly dependent on their help and active support after they had given up their homes and livelihood in Makkah. The Prophet described them as the particular favourites of *Allah* who will receive a splendid reward for their sacrifices vide Q2:218 "when those who have adopted the faith, who have migrated and fought for *Allah's* cause may hope for his grace." This was, however, at first only an indication of a future which had not yet materialized. The emigrants were held in high esteem because of their sacrifices and because of their connection in the teachings of Islam.

The Islamic calendar, Hijra started from the year of Hijrah from Makka to Medina in the year 622 AD.

[54] and [55]. Al-Hidayah Wal Dalal اَلْهِدَايَةُ وَالضَّلَالُ

Al-Hidayah means guidance. The word Hidayah is used in the *Quran* in the sense of guidance from *Allah* Q9:12 wherein *Allah* says guidance is Our concern.

The guidance is to the straight path[33] which the *Quran* calls the way of *Allah* and the path of the prophets and others blessed by Him. *Allah* guides man either directly through inspiration i.e. Ilqa or Ilham[62] or through inducement ie Taufiq[58]. He also guides man through the Wahi[61]. It is for the prophets to communicate the Divine message of guidance to people to act in an exemplary way to set up an example for others to follow. Apart from these ways of guidance *Allah* has instilled Divine guidance in the very instinct[51] of man by endowing him with the sense of distinguishing good from evil Q91:8.

Literal meaning of Al-Dalal is error. In the *Quran* Al-Dalal means that into which man falls by going astray from the straight path and by prefering to remain in the darkness of rank ignorance Q3:64 after the light of Divine guidance has reached him with the result that he refrains from taking to the right way of living ie Deen(15) and takes to wrong ways of life in defiance to the commandments of *Allah*. There are many Ayat of the *Quran* which cause an impression on the reader's mind just as *Allah* gives right guidance to man so also He guides him astray, depending on His own will; but if one takes into account all the Ayat relating to Dalalat it will be more than clear to him that when man takes the initiative in going Astray by his own will *Allah* lets him go Astray. In other words those who earn error as a matter of right, *Allah* lets them go astray since *Allah* does not behold anything from man what he earns by himself as his right, whether it is for his good or for his hurt Q7:30, 16:36.

Dalal Mubin means rank ignorance or flagrant error Q3:64. Dalal Bayid means wandering far Astray Q4:116.

[56]. Al-Nahiyu Anil Munkar اَلنَّهِيُ عَنِ الْمُنْكَرِ

Al-Nahiyu Anil Munkar is a combination of two words. Al-Nahi means to create or inculcate in the mind a sense or realization of decay, degradation or corruption. Al-Munkar means that which is corrupt. Awareness of wrong and injustice is an important ingredient of Iman(3). The prophet of Islam said "If any impropriety or injustice is committed in your presence remedy it with your hands. If it is not possible (due to strong opposition) then stop it with your tongue. If even that is not possible then realize in your mind that it is wrong. For that is the last grade of Iman. It therefore implies that nonrealization of wrong is the absence of Iman.

[57]. Al-Tawhid اَلتَّوْحِيْدُ

Monotheism or the unity of *Allah* is one of the fundamental principles of Al-Islam(20). Al-Quran[47] teaches uncompromising and pure monotheism ie *Allah* is All Powerful, Ruler and Master of all. He requires no partners nor has any offspring or family. He alone is worthy of worship. The basic testimony of Iman(3) is: *La Ilaha Il Allah*. This testimony implies that there is one *Allah* for the entire universe. It also implies that none has the right to be worshipped but *Allah*.

[58]. Al-Tawfiq اَلتَّوفِيق

The literal meaning of Al-Tawfiq is inducement or suggestion. In the *Quran* this word is used for Divine impulse. It is always related to a kind of inspiration that comes from *Allah* to His servant for doing successfully any good act which amounts to an accomplishment in the sight of *Allah*.

The word Tawfiq has been used in the *Quran* to convey different meaning in the context of the Ayat in which it is used. "If they desire a reconcillation *Allah* will make them of one mind" Q4:35.

"Accomplishment of my work (my striving) or my mission) rests with none but *Allah*" Q11:88.

"Whoso desires the life of the world and its attractions We pay them fully for their deeds therein" Q11:15.

Al-Tawfiq also means full recompence as in Q78:26.

[59]. Al-Waliy اَلوَلِيّ

Waliy means one who is very near. In the *Quran* Waliy applies to the favourites of *Allah* or to the holy men vide Q10:63 "Are not friends (Auliya) of *Allah* those for whom there is no fear Huzn (10). Awliya is plural of Wali.

The other derivatives from the root Wala are Maula meaning (a) nearly related (b) heir(c) sharer or partner. All the three meanings are implied in Q4:33 Mawla also means neighbor, friend, protector or client Q44:44. Mawla also means Lord, or master Q16:76. Mawali is plural of Mawla.

[60]. Ulul-Amr اُولِي الاَمر

Ulul Amr are those charged with responsibility, authority, decision and settlement of affairs. All ultimate authority vests in *Allah*. Men of *Allah* derive their authority from Him. Al-Islam(20) makes no sharp division between sacred and secular affairs. It expects ordinary governments to be imbued with righteousness and stand in the place of the righteous Imam. We must respect and obey such authority; otherwise there will be no order or discipline.

Amir, Amir-ul-Muminin, Imam[2] or Khalifah[22] are equivalent words.

[61] and [62]. Al-Wahiy-wal Ilham اَلْوَحْيُ وَالْاِلْهَامُ

The word Waha from which wahiy is derived occurs in a number of shades of meaning each indicating the under lying idea of inspiration, directing or guiding some one.

Wahiy in the sense of revelation is guidance from *Allah* for His creation, brought by the Rusul(17) who received it from *Allah* through one of the means mentioned in the *Quran* [48] "It is not fitting for a man that *Allah* should speak to him except by Wahiy or from behind a veil or by sending of a messenger to reveal with authority from *Allah* what *Allah* wills, for He is Most High, Most Wise" Q42:51.

Verbal signs (as against the natural signs [6]) are given directly only to one particular person, the prophet and only indirectly and mediately to mankind. In Islam, however, it is the verbal communication which is authentic.

Revelation is the most authentic source of information as it is the knowledge of the Creator who knows every detail of His creation. Revelation is the only such source of information whose validity cannot be questioned while other sources are liable to be tested, criticized and judged on the basis of Wahi.

Revelation is thus, the ultimate truth in the sense that any conclusion based on the application of one or the other method has got to be filtered through Revelation before final expression. In this very sense the *Quran* is called Al-Furqan[47]

Revelation is the part of *Allah*'s knowledge which has been conveyed to man through Rusul(17) at different stages of history. Seeming differences were found to suit existing situations. Fundamental values remained unchanged as any compromise on the basics was impossible.

Means of Wahiy are:

[a] Inspiration in a dream vide Q37:102.

[b] Speech hidden away vide Q27:8.

[c] Words [speech] conveyed through Angel Jibriel.

Ilham literally means to cause to swallow or gulp down. As distinct from Wahiy, Ilham means inspiration to pious men individually by knowledge cast into their minds. If the inspiration is cast to men in general by messages sent through the Rusul it is Wahiy. It differs from Wahiy in that the Wahiy is brought by the angel to the Rasul and it is communicated to men by the Rasul. Ilham is for the individual instruction of the recipient.

> Ilham differs from intellectual knowledge in that it cannot be gained by meditation and deduction; but is suddenly communicated while the recipient cannot tell how, whence or why. It is the pure gift from the generosity of *Allah*.

Ilham differs from Wasswass (satanic whispering) in respect of the things to which it incites - good as opposed to evil.

QURANIC FAVOURITES

1. In the name of Allah the Merciful the Mercy-giving.

بِسْمِ اللّٰهِ الرَّحْمٰنِ الرَّحِيْمِ

Surah 1

2. 1:1 Praise (obedience) to Allah, Sustainer (Rubb) of the universe.

اَلْحَمْدُ لِلّٰهِ رَبِّ الْعٰلَمِيْنَ

3. 1:5 Guide us to the Straight Path.

اِهْدِنَا الصِّرَاطَ الْمُسْتَقِيْمَ

Surah 2

4. 2:7 Allah has sealed their hearts and hearing and on their eyes there is a covering.

خَتَمَ اللّٰهُ عَلٰى قُلُوْبِهِمْ وَعَلٰى سَمْعِهِمْ

وَعَلٰٓى اَبْصَارِهِمْ غِشَاوَةٌ

5. 2:18 They are deaf, dumb and blind and cannot return.

صُمٌّ بُكْمٌ عُمْيٌ فَهُمْ لَا يَرْجِعُوْنَ

6.	2:19	Allah encompasses the disbelievers (kuffar).
		وَاللّٰهُ مُحِيْطٌ بِالْكٰفِرِيْنَ
7.	2:20	Allah is powerful over everything.
		إِنَّ اللّٰهَ عَلٰى كُلِّ شَىْءٍ قَدِيْرٌ
8.	2:23	If you are truthful, then produce a Sura of the like thereof, and call your witnesses besides Allah.
		فَأْتُوْا بِسُوْرَةٍ مِّنْ مِّثْلِهٖ ص وَادْعُوْا شُهَدَآءَكُمْ مِّنْ دُوْنِ اللّٰهِ إِنْ كُنْتُمْ صٰدِقِيْنَ
9.	2:27	Those are the ones who are the losers.
		أُولٰٓئِكَ هُمُ الْخٰسِرُوْنَ
10.	2:31	He (Allah) taught Adam all the names.
		وَعَلَّمَ اٰدَمَ الْأَسْمَآءَ كُلَّهَا
11.	2:37	He (Allah) is the relenting, the Mercy-giving.
		إِنَّهٗ هُوَ التَّوَّابُ الرَّحِيْمُ
12.	2:41	Bargain not My (Allah's) revelations for a trifling price.
		وَلَا تَشْتَرُوْا بِاٰيٰتِيْ ثَمَنًا قَلِيْلًا
13.	2:44	Do you enjoin righteousness upon mankind while you yourselves forget (to practice it)?
		أَتَأْمُرُوْنَ النَّاسَ بِالْبِرِّ وَتَنْسَوْنَ أَنْفُسَكُمْ

14. 2:45 **Seek help in patience (Sabr) and prayer (Salat).**

وَاسْتَعِيْنُوْا بِالصَّبْرِ وَالصَّلٰوةِ

15. 2:60 Eat and drink of that which Allah has provided and do not act corruptly as mischief mongers.

كُلُوْا وَاشْرَبُوْا مِنْ رِّزْقِ اللّٰهِ وَلَا تَعْثَوْا فِي الْاَرْضِ مُفْسِدِيْنَ

16. 2:62 No fear shall come upon them,neither shall they grieve.

وَلَا خَوْفٌ عَلَيْهِمْ وَلَا هُمْ يَحْزَنُوْنَ

17. 2:83 Speak kindly with people.

وَقُوْلُوْا لِلنَّاسِ حُسْنًا

18. 2:96 You will find them greediest of all for life.

وَلَتَجِدَنَّهُمْ اَحْرَصَ النَّاسِ عَلٰى حَيٰوةٍ

19. 2:105 Allah chooses for His Mercy whom He will.

وَاللّٰهُ يَخْتَصُّ بِرَحْمَتِهٖ مَنْ يَّشَآءُ

20. 2:105 Allah is of infinite bounty.

وَاللّٰهُ ذُو الْفَضْلِ الْعَظِيْمِ

21. 2:110 Whatever good (deeds) you send before for your souls (selves) you shall find it with Allah.

وَمَا تُقَدِّمُوْا لِاَنْفُسِكُمْ مِّنْ خَيْرٍ تَجِدُوْهُ عِنْدَ اللّٰهِ

22. 2:114 Who is greater oppressor than he who prohibits the recitation of the name of Allah in the mosques and strives for their ruin.

وَمَنْ أَظْلَمُ مِمَّنْ مَّنَعَ مَسَٰجِدَ اللَّهِ أَن يُذْكَرَ فِيهَا اسْمُهُ وَسَعَىٰ فِي خَرَابِهَا

23. 2:115 Whither soever you turn there is Allah's countenance.

فَأَيْنَمَا تُوَلُّوا فَثَمَّ وَجْهُ

24. 2:116 Whatsoever is in the heavens and the earth is His. All are obedient to Him.

بَل لَّهُ مَا فِي السَّمَٰوَٰتِ وَالْأَرْضِ

25. 2:121 Study it as it should be studied.

يَتْلُونَهُ حَقَّ تِلَاوَتِهِ

26. 2:132 Die not save as Muslim (those who are committed to Allah).

فَلَا تَمُوتُنَّ إِلَّا وَأَنتُم مُّسْلِمُونَ

27. 2:138 (We take our) color from Allah and who is better than Allah at coloring?

صِبْغَةَ اللَّهِ ج وَمَنْ أَحْسَنُ مِنَ اللَّهِ صِبْغَةً

28. 2:140 Say: Do you know better or does Allah?

قُلْ ءَأَنتُمْ أَعْلَمُ أَمِ اللَّهُ

29. 2:140 Allah is not unaware of what you do.

وَمَا اللَّهُ بِغَٰفِلٍ عَمَّا تَعْمَلُونَ

30. 2:148 Vie with one another in good deeds.

فَاسْتَبِقُوا الْخَيْرٰتِ

31. 2:152 Remember Me, I will remember you.

فَاذْكُرُوْنِيْٓ اَذْكُرْكُمْ وَاشْكُرُوْا لِيْ وَلَا تَكْفُرُوْنِ

32. 2:153 Allah is with those who have patience (Sabreen).

وَاللّٰهُ مَعَ الصّٰبِرِيْنَ

33. 2:156 We belong to Allah and to Him we will surely return.

اِنَّا لِلّٰهِ وَاِنَّآ اِلَيْهِ رٰجِعُوْنَ

34. 2:165 Those who believe are stauncher in their love for Allah.

وَالَّذِيْنَ اٰمَنُوْٓا اَشَدُّ حُبًّا لِّلّٰهِ

35. 2:168 O people! Eat of that which is lawful and wholesome in the earth and follow not the footsteps of the satan.

كُلُوْا مِمَّا فِي الْاَرْضِ حَلٰلًا طَيِّبًا ۡ وَّلَا تَتَّبِعُوْا خُطُوٰتِ الشَّيْطٰنِ

36. 2:168 He (Satan) is an open enemy for you.

اِنَّهٗ لَكُمْ عَدُوٌّ مُّبِيْنٌ

37. 2:173 Allah is forgiving,Mercy-giving.

اِنَّ اللّٰهَ غَفُوْرٌ رَّحِيْمٌ

38. 2:181 Allah is Hearer, Knower.

اِنَّ اللّٰهَ سَمِيْعٌ عَلِيْمٌ

39. 2:184 **Whoso willingly does a good work it shall be better for him.**

فَمَنْ تَطَوَّعَ خَيْرًا فَهُوَ خَيْرٌ لَّهُ

40. 2:188 Devour not wealth among yourselves by wrong means nor present it (as bribe) to judges.

وَلَا تَأْكُلُوٓا أَمْوَالَكُمْ بَيْنَكُمْ بِالْبَاطِلِ
وَتُدْلُوا بِهَآ إِلَى الْحُكَّامِ

41. 2:190 Allah loves not the transgressors.

إِنَّ اللّٰهَ لَا يُحِبُّ الْمُعْتَدِيْنَ

42. 2:191 Mischief making is worse than slaughter.

وَالْفِتْنَةُ أَشَدُّ مِنَ الْقَتْلِ

43. 2:194 Whoso then transgresses against you, you do transgress against him likewise (and no more).

فَمَنِ اعْتَدٰى عَلَيْكُمْ فَاعْتَدُوْا عَلَيْهِ
بِمِثْلِ مَا اعْتَدٰى عَلَيْكُمْ

44. 2:195 Allah loves those who do good (deeds).

إِنَّ اللّٰهَ يُحِبُّ الْمُحْسِنِيْنَ

45. 2:207 Allah has compassion on (His) bondmen.

وَاللّٰهُ رَءُوْفٌ بِالْعِبَادِ

46. 2:208 Come all of you ,into Islam and follow not the footsteps of the devil.

ادْخُلُوْا فِي السِّلْمِ كَآفَّةً ۠ وَّلَا تَتَّبِعُوْا خُطُوٰتِ الشَّيْطٰنِ

47. 2:216 It may happen that you hate a thing which is good for you and it may happen that you love a thing which is bad for you.

وَعَسٰٓى اَنْ تَكْرَهُوْا شَيْـًٔا وَّهُوَ خَيْرٌ لَّكُمْ

48. 2:222 Allah loves those who repent and loves those who are clean.

اِنَّ اللّٰهَ يُحِبُّ التَّوَّابِيْنَ وَيُحِبُّ الْمُتَطَهِّرِيْنَ

49. 2:225 Allah is forgiving, Clement.

وَاللّٰهُ غَفُوْرٌ حَلِيْمٌ

50. 2:229 These are the limits (imposed by Allah). Transgress them not.

تِلْكَ حُدُوْدُ اللّٰهِ فَلَا تَعْتَدُوْهَا

51. 2:231 Make not the revelations of Allah a laughing stock (by your behaviour).

وَلَا تَتَّخِذُوْٓا اٰيٰتِ اللّٰهِ هُزُوًا

52. 2:231 Observe your duty to Allah and know that Allah, is aware of all things.

وَاتَّقُوا اللّٰهَ وَاعْلَمُوْٓا اَنَّ اللّٰهَ بِكُلِّ شَيْءٍ عَلِيْمٌ

53. 2:237 If you forgive, it is nearer to piety.

وَاَنْ تَعْفُوْٓا اَقْرَبُ لِلتَّقْوٰى

54.	2:237	Forget not to be kind among yourselves.
		وَلَا تَنسَوُا الْفَضْلَ بَيْنَكُمْ
55.	2:238	Stand up with devotion before Allah.
		وَقُومُوا لِلَّهِ قَٰنِتِينَ
56.	2:247	Allah bestows His Sovereignty on whom He pleases.
		وَاللَّهُ يُؤْتِي مُلْكَهُ مَن يَشَاءُ
57	2:249	How often a small group has overcome a larger group with Allah's leave.
		كَم مِّن فِئَةٍ قَلِيلَةٍ غَلَبَتْ فِئَةً كَثِيرَةً بِإِذْنِ اللَّهِ
58.	2:251	Allah is the Lord of kindness over the universe.
		وَلَٰكِنَّ اللَّهَ ذُو فَضْلٍ عَلَى الْعَٰلَمِينَ
59.	2:255	Allah! There is no god save Him, the Alive, the Eternal.
		اللَّهُ لَا إِلَٰهَ إِلَّا هُوَ الْحَيُّ الْقَيُّومُ
60.	2:256	There is no compulsion in religion (deen).
		لَا إِكْرَاهَ فِي الدِّينِ
61.	2:257	Allah is the protecting Friend of those who believe. He brings them out of darkness into light.
		اللَّهُ وَلِيُّ الَّذِينَ آمَنُوا يُخْرِجُهُم مِّنَ الظُّلُمَٰتِ إِلَى النُّورِ

62. 2:261 Allah gives manifold increase to whom He please. Allah is All Embracing, All Knowing.

وَاللّٰهُ يُضٰعِفُ لِمَنْ يَّشَآءُ ۗ وَاللّٰهُ وَاسِعٌ عَلِيْمٌ

63. 2:273 Whatsoever goc d thing you spend, Allah knows it.

وَمَا تُنْفِقُوْا مِنْ خَيْرٍ فَاِنَّ اللّٰهَ بِهٖ عَلِيْمٌ

64. 2:282 When you contract debt for a fixed term record it in writing.

اِذَا تَدَايَنْتُمْ بِدَيْنٍ اِلٰٓى اَجَلٍ مُّسَمًّى فَاكْتُبُوْهُ

65. 2:283 Hide not testimony.

وَلَا تَكْتُمُوا الشَّهَادَةَ

66. 2:284 Whatsoever is in the heavens and whatsoever is in the earth (belongs) to Allah.

لِلّٰهِ مَا فِي السَّمٰوٰتِ وَمَا فِي الْاَرْضِ

67. 2:286 Allah burdens not a soul beyond its capacity.

لَا يُكَلِّفُ اللّٰهُ نَفْسًا اِلَّا وُسْعَهَا

68. 2:286 For it (is only)that which it has earned.

لَهَا مَا كَسَبَتْ وَعَلَيْهَا مَا اكْتَسَبَتْ

69. 2:286 Our Lord condemns us not if we forget or miss the mark.

رَبَّنَا لَا تُؤَاخِذْنَآ اِنْ نَّسِيْنَآ اَوْ اَخْطَاْنَا

70.	2:286	Our Lord! Lay not on us such a burden as you did lay on those before us.

رَبَّنَا وَلَا تَحْمِلْ عَلَيْنَآ إِصْرًا كَمَا حَمَلْتَهُ
عَلَى الَّذِينَ مِن قَبْلِنَا

71.	2:286	Our Lord! Impose not on us that which we have not the strength to bear.

رَبَّنَا وَلَا تُحَمِّلْنَا مَا لَا طَاقَةَ لَنَا بِهِ

72.	2:286	Pardon us,absolve us and have mercy on us. Thou our Protcctor! and give us victory over the disbelieving people (Kuffar).

وَاعْفُ عَنَّا وَاغْفِرْ لَنَا وَارْحَمْنَا
أَنتَ مَوْلَىٰنَا فَانصُرْنَا عَلَى الْقَوْمِ الْكَافِرِينَ

Surah 3

73.	3:7	But only the men of understanding really heed.

وَمَا يَذَّكَّرُ إِلَّآ أُولُوا الْأَلْبَابِ

74.	3:19	Religion with Allah is commitment to His Will and Guidance (Islam).

إِنَّ الدِّينَ عِندَ اللَّهِ الْإِسْلَامُ

75.	3:19	Whoso disbelieves the revelations of Allah (will find that) Allah is swift at reckoning.

وَمَن يَكْفُرْ بِآيَاتِ اللَّهِ فَإِنَّ اللَّهَ سَرِيعُ الْحِسَابِ

76. 3:20 If they accept Islam, then truly they are rightly guided.

فَإِنْ أَسْلَمُوا فَقَدِ اهْتَدَوْا

77. 3:27 (Allah) you give unlimited subsistence to whom You please.

وَتَرْزُقُ مَنْ تَشَاءُ بِغَيْرِ حِسَابٍ

78. 3:32 Obey Allah and the Messenger.

وَأَطِيعُوا اللَّهَ وَالرَّسُولَ

79. 3:48 He (Allah) will teach him (Jesus) the Book and Wisdom, the Taurat (Torah) and the Injil (Gospel).

وَيُعَلِّمُهُ الْكِتٰبَ وَالْحِكْمَةَ وَالتَّوْرٰىةَ وَالْإِنْجِيلَ

80. 3:77 As for those who sell the covenant of (faith they owe to Allah) and their own oaths (agreements) for a petty price.

إِنَّ الَّذِينَ يَشْتَرُونَ بِعَهْدِ اللَّهِ
وَأَيْمَانِهِمْ ثَمَنًا قَلِيلًا

81. 3:84 We make no distinction between any of them (His messengers) and we are commited to Him (Allah) alone.

لَا نُفَرِّقُ بَيْنَ أَحَدٍ مِنْهُمْ
وَنَحْنُ لَهُ مُسْلِمُونَ

82. 3:85 Whoso seeks as religion other than Islam, it will not be accepted from him.

وَمَنْ يَبْتَغِ غَيْرَ الْإِسْلَامِ دِينًا فَلَنْ يُقْبَلَ مِنْهُ

83. 3:86 Allah guides not wrong doing folk.

وَاللّٰهُ لَا يَهْدِي الْقَوْمَ الظّٰلِمِيْنَ

84. 3:92 You will not attain piety unless you spend that which you cherish.

لَنْ تَنَالُوا الْبِرَّ حَتّٰى تُنْفِقُوْا مِمَّا تُحِبُّوْنَ ۵

85. 3:95 Follow the religion of Ibrahim (Abraham) the upright. He was not of the idolators.

فَاتَّبِعُوْا مِلَّةَ اِبْرٰهِيْمَ حَنِيْفًا

وَمَا كَانَ مِنَ الْمُشْرِكِيْنَ

86. 3:103 Hold fast all of you together to the rope of Allah and be not divided.

وَاعْتَصِمُوْا بِحَبْلِ اللّٰهِ جَمِيْعًا وَّلَا تَفَرَّقُوْا

87. 3:110 You are the best community that has been raised up for mankind. You enjoin right conduct and forbid indecency.

كُنْتُمْ خَيْرَ اُمَّةٍ اُخْرِجَتْ لِلنَّاسِ

تَاْمُرُوْنَ بِالْمَعْرُوْفِ وَتَنْهَوْنَ عَنِ الْمُنْكَرِ

88. 3:119 Allah is aware of what is hidden in(your breasts).

اِنَّ اللّٰهَ عَلِيْمٌ بِذَاتِ الصُّدُوْرِ

89. 3:122 In Allah do believers put their trust.

وَعَلَى اللّٰهِ فَلْيَتَوَكَّلِ الْمُؤْمِنُوْنَ

90. 3:134 Those who control their wrath and pardon (all) men.

وَالْكٰظِمِيْنَ الْغَيْظَ وَالْعَافِيْنَ عَنِ النَّاسِ

91. 3:140 These are ayyam (days) which We cause to rotate between mankind.

وَتِلْكَ الْاَيَّامُ نُدَاوِلُهَا بَيْنَ النَّاسِ

92. 3:160 If Allah is your helper none can overcome you.

اِنْ يَّنْصُرْكُمُ اللّٰهُ فَلَا غَالِبَ لَكُمْ

93. 3:173 Allah is sufficient for us. He is the Most Excellent in whom we trust.

حَسْبُنَا اللّٰهُ وَنِعْمَ الْوَكِيْلُ

94. 3:180 The heritage of the heavens and the earth is for Allah.

وَلِلّٰهِ مِيْرَاثُ السَّمٰوٰتِ وَالْاَرْضِ

95. 3:185 Every life will have taste of death.

كُلُّ نَفْسٍ ذَآئِقَةُ الْمَوْتِ

96. 3:185 The life of this world is nothing but comfort of illusion.

وَمَا الْحَيٰوةُ الدُّنْيَآ اِلَّا مَتَاعُ الْغُرُوْرِ

97. 3:189 Unto Allah belongs the Sovereignty of the heavens and the earth.

وَلِلّٰهِ مُلْكُ السَّمٰوٰتِ وَالْاَرْضِ

98. 3:191 Our Rubb! You have not created this (universe) in vain.

رَبَّنَا مَا خَلَقْتَ هٰذَا بَاطِلًا

99. 3:195 Reward is from Allah and with Allah is the fairest of rewards.

ثَوَابًا مِّنْ عِنْدِ اللّٰهِ وَاللّٰهُ عِنْدَهٗ حُسْنُ الثَّوَابِ

100. 3:133 Hasten for forgiveness from your Lord.

وَسَارِعُوْٓا اِلٰى مَغْفِرَةٍ مِّنْ رَّبِّكُمْ

urah 4

101. 4:45 Allah is sufficient as a helper.

وَكَفٰى بِاللّٰهِ وَلِيًّا

102. 4:59 That is better and more seemly in the end.

ذٰلِكَ خَيْرٌ وَّ اَحْسَنُ تَاْوِيْلًا

103. 4:69 The best of company are they.

وَحَسُنَ اُولٰٓئِكَ رَفِيْقًا

104. 4:78 Say to them: All is from Allah.

قُلْ كُلٌّ مِّنْ عِنْدِ اللّٰهِ

105. 4:82 Why don't they ponder on the Quran.

اَفَلَا يَتَدَبَّرُوْنَ الْقُرْاٰنَ

106. 4:85 Whoso intervenes (recommends) in a good cause will have the reward thereof.

مَنْ يَّشْفَعْ شَفَاعَةً حَسَنَةً يَّكُنْ لَّهٗ نَصِيْبٌ مِّنْهَا

107. 4:116 Whoso joins partners with Allah has wandered far astray.

وَمَنْ يُّشْرِكْ بِاللّٰهِ فَقَدْ ضَلَّ ضَلٰلًا بَعِيْدًا

108. 4:139 All power belongs to Allah.

فَإِنَّ الْعِزَّةَ لِلَّهِ جَمِيعًا

109. 4:157 They have no knowledge thereof save (except) pursuit of a conjecture.

مَا لَهُمْ بِهِ مِنْ عِلْمٍ إِلَّا اتِّبَاعَ الظَّنِّ

110. 4:169 That is very easy for Allah.

وَكَانَ ذَٰلِكَ عَلَى اللَّهِ يَسِيرًا

111. 4:171 Do not utter anything concerning Allah except the truth.

وَلَا تَقُولُوا عَلَى اللَّهِ إِلَّا الْحَقَّ

Surah 5

112. 5:1 O Believers! Fulfill your undertakings (agreements).

يَا أَيُّهَا الَّذِينَ آمَنُوا أَوْفُوا بِالْعُقُودِ

113. 5:2 Seeking the grace and pleasure of Allah.

يَبْتَغُونَ فَضْلًا مِنْ رَبِّهِمْ وَرِضْوَانًا

114. 5:2 Help one another in righteousness and piety.

وَتَعَاوَنُوا عَلَى الْبِرِّ وَالتَّقْوَىٰ

115. 5:2 Fear (keep your duty to) Allah! Allah is severe in punishment.

وَاتَّقُوا اللَّهَ إِنَّ اللَّهَ شَدِيدُ الْعِقَابِ

116. 5:54 Such is the Grace of Allah which He gives to whom He wishes. Allah is All Embracing, All Knowing.

ذٰلِكَ فَضْلُ اللّٰهِ يُؤْتِيهِ مَنْ
يَشَآءُ ۚ وَاللّٰهُ وَاسِعٌ عَلِيمٌ

117. 5:55 Your friend can be only Allah, and His Messenger (Rasul) and those who have faith (Muminun).

إِنَّمَا وَلِيُّكُمُ اللّٰهُ وَرَسُولُهُ وَالَّذِينَ اٰمَنُوا

118. 5:57 If you are true believers (Muminun) fear (be dutiful to) Allah.

وَاتَّقُوا اللّٰهَ إِنْ كُنْتُمْ مُّؤْمِنِينَ

119. 5:73 There is no god (ilah) except the one God.

وَمَا مِنْ إِلٰهٍ إِلَّآ إِلٰهٌ وَّاحِدٌ

120. 5:88 Eat of that which Allah has bestowed on you as food, lawful and wholesome, and be fearful (dutiful) to Allah in whom you have faith.

وَكُلُوا مِمَّا رَزَقَكُمُ اللّٰهُ حَلٰلًا طَيِّبًا
وَّاتَّقُوا اللّٰهَ الَّذِيٓ أَنْتُمْ بِهِ مُؤْمِنُونَ

121. 5:89 Take care of your oaths (agreements).

وَاحْفَظُوٓا أَيْمَانَكُمْ

122. 5:99 The duty of the messenger (Rasul) is nothing except to convey (the message).

مَا عَلَى الرَّسُولِ إِلَّا الْبَلٰغُ

123. 5:120 To Allah belongs the Sovereignty of the heavens and the earth and whatsoever is therein.

لِلّٰهِ مُلْكُ السَّمٰوٰتِ وَالْاَرْضِ وَمَا فِيْهِنَّ

Surah 6

124. 6:20 They (to whom we gave scripture) recognise (this Prophet) as they recognise their sons.

يَعْرِفُوْنَهٗ كَمَا يَعْرِفُوْنَ اَبْنَآءَهُمْ

125. 6:32 The life of the world is naught except a pastime and sport.

وَمَا الْحَيٰوةُ الدُّنْيَآ اِلَّا لَعِبٌ وَّلَهْوٌ

126. 6:46 Who is the god (ilah) who could restore them (the bounties) to you except Allah?

مَنْ اِلٰهٌ غَيْرُ اللّٰهِ يَاْتِيْكُمْ بِهٖ

127. 6:57 The decision (order) is for Allah only.

اِنِ الْحُكْمُ اِلَّا لِلّٰهِ

128. 6:59 Not a leaf falls but He knows it.

وَمَا تَسْقُطُ مِنْ وَّرَقَةٍ اِلَّا يَعْلَمُهَا

129. 6:71 The guidance of Allah is (alone the) Guidance.

قُلْ اِنَّ هُدَى اللّٰهِ هُوَ الْهُدٰى

130. 6:72 Establish worship (salat) and fear (be dutiful to) Him.

وَاَنْ اَقِيْمُوا الصَّلٰوةَ وَاتَّقُوْهُ

131. 6:93 They are careful of their worship (salat).

وَهُمْ عَلَىٰ صَلَاتِهِمْ يُحَافِظُونَ

132. 6:100 Glorified be He and high exalted above (all) than what they ascribe (to Him).

سُبْحَٰنَهُ وَتَعَٰلَىٰ عَمَّا يَصِفُونَ

133. 6:106 Turn away from those who join others with Allah (mushrikin).

وَأَعْرِضْ عَنِ الْمُشْرِكِينَ

134. 6:142 Be not prodigal. Allah loves not the prodigals.

وَلَا تُسْرِفُوا ۚ إِنَّهُ لَا يُحِبُّ الْمُسْرِفِينَ

135. 6:148 Say: Your Lord (Rubb) is of embracing mercy.

فَقُلْ رَّبُّكُمْ ذُو رَحْمَةٍ وَّاسِعَةٍ

136. 6:150 Say: With Allah is the final argument.

قُلْ فَلِلَّهِ الْحُجَّةُ الْبَالِغَةُ

137. 6:154 This is My straight path (Sirat-al Mustaqim) so follw it.

وَأَنَّ هَٰذَا صِرَاطِي مُسْتَقِيمًا فَاتَّبِعُوهُ

138. 6:159 Say:You wait we (too) are waiting.

قُلِ انْتَظِرُوا إِنَّا مُنْتَظِرُونَ

139. 6:165 No laden shall bear another's load.

وَلَا تَزِرُ وَازِرَةٌ وِّزْرَ أُخْرَىٰ

140. 7:3 You pay little heed (to guidance).

قَلِيلًا مَّا تَذَكَّرُونَ

141. 7:17 You will not find most of them thankful (to you).

وَلَا تَجِدُ أَكْثَرَهُمْ شَٰكِرِينَ

142. 7:23 They (Adam and Eve) said: Our Lord! (Rubb) We have wronged ourselves.

قَالَا رَبَّنَا ظَلَمْنَآ أَنفُسَنَا

143. 7:28 Allah enjoins not lewdness.

إِنَّ ٱللَّهَ لَا يَأْمُرُ بِٱلْفَحْشَآءِ

144. 7:29 Say: My Lord (Rubb)enjoins justice.

قُلْ أَمَرَ رَبِّى بِٱلْقِسْطِ

145. 7:34 Every nation has its term.

وَلِكُلِّ أُمَّةٍ أَجَلٌ

146. 7:34 When its (nation's) time comes it cannot put it off an hour nor can it advance it.

فَإِذَا جَآءَ أَجَلُهُمْ لَا يَسْتَأْخِرُونَ سَاعَةً
وَلَا يَسْتَقْدِمُونَ

147. 7:35 Whosoever refrain from evil and amend, no fear shall come upon them neither shall they grieve.

فَمَنِ اتَّقٰى وَاَصْلَحَ فَلَا خَوْفٌ عَلَيْهِمْ
وَلَا هُمْ يَحْزَنُوْنَ

148. 7:47 They will say: "Our Lord! (Rubb) place us not with the wrong doing folk."

قَالُوْا رَبَّنَا لَا تَجْعَلْنَا مَعَ الْقَوْمِ الظّٰلِمِيْنَ

149. 7:49 Enter the garden. No fear shall come upon you nor is it you who will grieve.

اُدْخُلُوا الْجَنَّةَ لَاخَوْفٌ عَلَيْكُمْ وَلَآ اَنْتُمْ تَحْزَنُوْنَ

150. 7:54 All creation and commandment are His. Blessed be Allah the Lord (Rubb) of the universe.

اَلَا لَهُ الْخَلْقُ وَالْاَمْرُ
تَبٰرَكَ اللّٰهُ رَبُّ الْعٰلَمِيْنَ

151. 7:56 Create not confusion on earth after (establishment of) order.

وَلَا تُفْسِدُوْا فِي الْاَرْضِ بَعْدَ اِصْلَاحِهَا

152. 7:68 I am for you a true adviser.

وَاَنَا لَكُمْ نَاصِحٌ اَمِيْنٌ

153. 7:69 Remember (all) the bounties of Allah, that you may be successful.

فَاذْكُرُوْٓا اٰلَآءَ اللّٰهِ لَعَلَّكُمْ تُفْلِحُوْنَ

154. 7:79 You love not (good) advisers.

وَلَٰكِن لَّا تُحِبُّونَ النَّٰصِحِينَ

155. 7:86 Remember, when you were but few, how He did multiply you.

وَاذْكُرُوٓا إِذْ كُنتُمْ قَلِيلًا فَكَثَّرَكُمْ

156. 7:89 In Allah do we put our trust.

عَلَى اللَّهِ تَوَكَّلْنَا

157. 7:99 Are they then safe from Allah's design?

أَفَأَمِنُوا مَكْرَ اللَّهِ

158. 7:126 Our Lord! (Rubb) vouchsafe us steadfastness, make us die as Muslims (men committed to you).

رَبَّنَآ أَفْرِغْ عَلَيْنَا صَبْرًا وَتَوَفَّنَا مُسْلِمِينَ

159. 7:128 Seek help from Allah and (wait) in patience.

اسْتَعِينُوا بِاللَّهِ وَاصْبِرُوا

160. 7:150 Make not my enemies ridicule me.

فَلَا تُشْمِتْ بِيَ الْأَعْدَآءَ

161. 7:157 He (Prophet) will relieve them of their burdens and the fetters that they used to wear.

وَيَضَعُ عَنْهُمْ إِصْرَهُمْ وَالْأَغْلَٰلَ الَّتِي كَانَتْ عَلَيْهِمْ

162. 7:169 (An unworthy) generation has succeeded them who inherited the scriptures.

فَخَلَفَ مِنۢ بَعْدِهِمْ خَلْفٌ

163. 7:169 Shall not speak aught concerning Allah except the truth.

أَن لَّا يَقُولُوا عَلَى اللَّهِ إِلَّا الْحَقَّ

164. 7:172 Am I not your Lord (Rubb)? They said: Yes (You are).

أَلَسْتُ بِرَبِّكُمْ ۖ قَالُوا بَلَىٰ

165. 7:178 He whom Allah leads,is rightly guided.

مَن يَهْدِ اللَّهُ فَهُوَ الْمُهْتَدِي

166. 7:179 They have hearts wherewith they understand not.

لَهُمْ قُلُوبٌ لَّا يَفْقَهُونَ بِهَا

167. 7:179 They are like cattle - nay but they are worse.

أُولَٰئِكَ كَالْأَنْعَامِ بَلْ هُمْ أَضَلُّ

168. 7:180 Allah's are the fairest names. Invoke Him by them.

وَلِلَّهِ الْأَسْمَاءُ الْحُسْنَىٰ فَادْعُوهُ بِهَا

169. 7:189 He it is Who did create you from a single soul.

هُوَ الَّذِي خَلَقَكُم مِّن نَّفْسٍ وَاحِدَةٍ

170. 7:199 Keep to forgiveness (O Muhammed) and enjoin kindness and turn away (avoid) from the ignorant.

خُذِ الْعَفْوَ وَأْمُرْ بِالْعُرْفِ وَأَعْرِضْ
عَنِ الْجَاهِلِينَ

171. 8:1 Be fearful to Allah and adjust the matter of your difference.

فَاتَّقُوا اللّٰهَ وَاَصْلِحُوْا ذَاتَ بَيْنِكُمْ

172. 8:2 They alone are the true believers (Muminin) whose hearts fear when Allah is mentioned.

اِنَّمَا الْمُؤْمِنُوْنَ الَّذِيْنَ اِذَا ذُكِرَ اللّٰهُ
وَجِلَتْ قُلُوْبُهُمْ

173. 8:8 (That He might) cause the truth to triumph and bring vanity to naught.

لِيُحِقَّ الْحَقَّ وَيُبْطِلَ الْبَاطِلَ

174. 8:10 There is no victory except by the help of Allah.

وَمَا النَّصْرُ اِلَّا مِنْ عِنْدِ اللّٰهِ

175. 8:28 Know that your possessions and your children are a test.

وَاعْلَمُوْٓا اَنَّمَآ اَمْوَالُكُمْ وَاَوْلَادُكُمْ فِتْنَةٌ

176. 8:40 If they turn away, then know that Allah is your friend, a transcendent Helper.

وَاِنْ تَوَلَّوْا فَاعْلَمُوْٓا اَنَّ اللّٰهَ مَوْلٰىكُمْ ط
نِعْمَ الْمَوْلٰى وَنِعْمَ النَّصِيْرُ

177. 8:49 Whoso puts his trust in Allah (will find that) Allah is Mighty, Wise.

وَمَنْ يَتَوَكَّلْ عَلَى اللهِ فَإِنَّ اللهَ عَزِيزٌ حَكِيمٌ

178. 8:60 Whom you know not, Allah knows them.

لَا تَعْلَمُونَهُمُ اللهُ يَعْلَمُهُمْ

179. 8:72 If they seek help from you in the matter of religion, (Din) it is your duty to help (them).

وَإِنِ اسْتَنْصَرُوكُمْ فِي الدِّينِ فَعَلَيْكُمُ النَّصْرُ

Surah 9

180. 9:13 Allah has more right that you should fear Him if you are believers (Muminun).

فَاللهُ أَحَقُّ أَنْ تَخْشَوْهُ إِنْ كُنْتُمْ مُؤْمِنِينَ

181. 9:18 He only shall tend Allah's mosques who believes Allah and the last Day (of judgement).

مَنْ آمَنَ بِاللهِ وَالْيَوْمِ الْآخِرِ

إِنَّمَا يَعْمُرُ مَسٰجِدَ اللهِ

182. 9:31 There is no god save Him. He is above all that they ascribe as His Partners.

لَآ إِلٰهَ إِلَّا هُوَ سُبْحٰنَهُ عَمَّا يُشْرِكُونَ

183. 9:32 They wish (in vain) to put out the light of Allah with their mouths.

يُرِيدُونَ أَنْ يُطْفِئُوا نُورَ اللهِ بِأَفْوَاهِهِمْ

184. 9:40 Grieve not. Allah is with us.

لَا تَحْزَنْ إِنَّ اللّٰهَ مَعَنَا

185. 9:40 Allah's word it was that became the uppermost.

وَكَلِمَةُ اللّٰهِ هِيَ الْعُلْيَا

186. 9:54 (They) pay not (their contribution) save reluctantly.

وَلَا يُنْفِقُونَ إِلَّا وَهُمْ كٰرِهُونَ

187. 9:67 They forget Allah, so He has forgotten them.

نَسُوا اللّٰهَ فَنَسِيَهُمْ

188. 9:82 Let them laugh a little: They will weep much.

فَلْيَضْحَكُوا قَلِيلًا وَّلْيَبْكُوا كَثِيرًا

189. 9:94 He will tell you what you used to do.

فَيُنَبِّئُكُمْ بِمَا كُنْتُمْ تَعْمَلُونَ

190. 9:96 Allah accepts not wrong doing folk (fasiqin).

فَإِنَّ اللّٰهَ لَا يَرْضٰى عَنِ الْقَوْمِ الْفٰسِقِينَ

191. 9:99 Allah will soon bring them into His mercy.

سَيُدْخِلُهُمُ اللّٰهُ فِي رَحْمَتِهِ

192. 9:100 Allah is well pleased with them and they are well pleased with Him.

رَّضِيَ اللّٰهُ عَنْهُمْ وَرَضُوا عَنْهُ

193. 9:102 It may be that Allah will soon relent towards them.

عَسَى اللّٰهُ اَنْ يَّتُوْبَ عَلَيْهِمْ

194. 9:103 Your prayer (salat) is tranquility to them.

اِنَّ صَلٰوتَكَ سَكَنٌ لَّهُمْ

195. 9:111 Who fulfils the covenant better than Allah?

وَمَنْ اَوْفٰى بِعَهْدِهٖ مِنَ اللّٰهِ

196. 9:118 Allah is the Relenting,the Merciful.

اِنَّ اللّٰهَ هُوَ التَّوَّابُ الرَّحِيْمُ

197. 9:120 With Allah there is no loss of reward for those who do good.

اِنَّ اللّٰهَ لَا يُضِيْعُ اَجْرَ الْمُحْسِنِيْنَ

198. 9:123 Know that Allah is with those who fear to do wrong (Muttaqin).

وَاعْلَمُوْٓا اَنَّ اللّٰهَ مَعَ الْمُتَّقِيْنَ

199. 9:128 It is grieveous to him (the prophet) that you come to sorrow: He is full of concern for you (and) kind (and) merciful for the believers.

عَزِيْزٌ عَلَيْهِ مَا عَنِتُّمْ حَرِيْصٌ
عَلَيْكُمْ بِالْمُؤْمِنِيْنَ رَءُوْفٌ رَّحِيْمٌ

Surah 10

200. 10:22 It is He Who enable you to travel in the land and the sea.

هُوَ الَّذِىْ يُسَيِّرُكُمْ فِى الْبَرِّ وَالْبَحْرِ

201. 10:25 Allah calls(you) to the abode of peace.

وَاللّٰهُ يَدْعُوْٓا اِلٰى دَارِ السَّلٰمِ

202. 10:39 See what was the end of the wrong doers.

فَانْظُرْ كَيْفَ كَانَ عَاقِبَةُ الظّٰلِمِيْنَ

203. 10:47 For every people there is a messenger.

وَلِكُلِّ اُمَّةٍ رَّسُوْلٌ

204. 10:56 He gives life and gives death and to Him you wil be returned.

هُوَ يُحْيٖ وَيُمِيْتُ وَاِلَيْهِ تُرْجَعُوْنَ

205. 10:60 Truly Allah is full of grace to men but most of them are not thankful.

اِنَّ اللّٰهَ لَذُوْ فَضْلٍ عَلَى النَّاسِ
وَلٰكِنَّ اَكْثَرَهُمْ لَا يَشْكُرُوْنَ

206. 10:64 There is no change in the words (principles) of Allah.

لَا تَبْدِيْلَ لِكَلِمٰتِ اللّٰهِ

207. 10:81 Allah will not uphold the work of evil doers.

اِنَّ اللّٰهَ لَا يُصْلِحُ عَمَلَ الْمُفْسِدِيْنَ

208. 10:82 Allah will verify the truth by His words, however much the guilty (wicked) be averse.

وَيُحِقُّ اللّٰهُ الْحَقَّ بِكَلِمٰتِهٖ وَلَوْ كَرِهَ الْمُجْرِمُوْنَ

209. 10:85 O our Lord! (Rubb) Make us not trial for the wrong doing people (zalimin).

رَبَّنَا لَا تَجْعَلْنَا فِتْنَةً لِّلْقَوْمِ الظّٰلِمِيْنَ

210. 10:86 Save us by thy mercy from the wrong doing people (kafirun).

وَنَجِّنَا بِرَحْمَتِكَ مِنَ الْقَوْمِ الْكٰفِرِيْنَ

211. 10:103 It is incumbent (a duty) upon Us to save the believers (muminun).

حَقًّا عَلَيْنَا نُنْجِ الْمُؤْمِنِيْنَ

212. 10:108 Whosoever is guided is guided only for (the good of) his own soul (nafs).

فَمَنِ اهْتَدٰى فَاِنَّمَا يَهْتَدِىْ لِنَفْسِهٖ

Surah 11

213. 11:6 There is no moving thing on earth (beast, cattle) but the sustenance thereof depends on Allah.

وَمَا مِنْ دَآبَّةٍ فِى الْاَرْضِ اِلَّا عَلَى اللّٰهِ رِزْقُهَا

214. 11:18 Who does a greater wrong than he who invents a lie against Allah.

وَمَنْ اَظْلَمُ مِمَّنِ افْتَرٰى عَلَى اللّٰهِ كَذِبًا

215. 11:26 That you serve none but Allah.

اَنْ لَّا تَعْبُدُوْٓا اِلَّا اللّٰهَ

216. 11:41 In the name of Allah be its (Noah's Ark's) sailing and its anchoring. My Lord (Rubb) is oft forgiving, Mercy-giving.

بِسْمِ اللّٰهِ مَجْرٖىهَا وَمُرْسٰىهَا
إِنَّ رَبِّي لَغَفُورٌ رَّحِيمٌ

217. 11:49 Preserve patiently; the sequel is for those who fear to do wrong.

فَاصْبِرْ ۛ إِنَّ الْعَاقِبَةَ لِلْمُتَّقِينَ

218. 11:56 I rely upon (put my trust in) Allah, my sustainer (Rubb) and (also) your sustainer (Rubb).

إِنِّي تَوَكَّلْتُ عَلَى اللّٰهِ رَبِّي وَرَبِّكُمْ

219. 11:81 Their appointed time (tryst) is the morning. Is not the morning nigh?

إِنَّ مَوْعِدَهُمُ الصُّبْحُ ۚ أَلَيْسَ الصُّبْحُ بِقَرِيبٍ

220. 11:85 Give just measure and weight and diminish not to men (anything of) their goods.

أَوْفُوا الْمِكْيَالَ وَالْمِيزَانَ بِالْقِسْطِ
وَلَا تَبْخَسُوا النَّاسَ أَشْيَاءَهُمْ

221. 11:88 I desire nothing but reform, as far as I can.

إِنْ أُرِيدُ إِلَّا الْإِصْلَاحَ مَا اسْتَطَعْتُ

222. 11:88 There is no impulse (taufiq) for me but from Allah.

وَمَا تَوْفِيقِي إِلَّا بِاللّٰهِ

223. 11:123 Thy Lord (Rubb) is not unaware (unmindful) of what you (mortals) do.

وَمَا رَبُّكَ بِغَافِلٍ عَمَّا تَعْمَلُونَ

Surah 12

224. 12:21 Allah prevails over all His affairs.

وَاللَّهُ غَالِبٌ عَلَىٰٓ أَمْرِهِ

225. 12:51 We do not know any ill of him.

حَاشَ لِلَّهِ مَا عَلِمْنَا عَلَيْهِ مِن سُوٓءٍ

226. 12:67 In Him do I put my trust and in Him let all the trusting put their trust.

عَلَيْهِ تَوَكَّلْتُ وَعَلَيْهِ فَلْيَتَوَكَّلِ الْمُتَوَكِّلُونَ

227. 12:76 We raise by grades, whom We please.

نَرْفَعُ دَرَجٰتٍ مَّن نَّشَآءُ

228. 12:76 Above every one endowed with (degrees of exellence) knowledge there is one who knows better.

وَفَوْقَ كُلِّ ذِى عِلْمٍ عَلِيمٌ

229. 12:86 I only complain of my emotion and my grief to Allah.

إِنَّمَآ أَشْكُوا بَثِّى وَحُزْنِىٓ إِلَى اللَّهِ

230. 12:87 None despair of mercy of Allah except the disbelieving folk (kafirun).

إِنَّهُ لَا يَايْئَسُ مِن رَّوْحِ اللَّهِ إِلَّا الْقَوْمُ الْكٰفِرُونَ

231. 12:88 Allah will reward the charitable (Mutasadiqin).

إِنَّ اللّٰهَ يَجْزِي الْمُتَصَدِّقِينَ

232. 12:101 You are my patron in this world and the hereafter.

أَنْتَ وَلِيِّ فِي الدُّنْيَا وَالْآخِرَةِ

233. 12:101 Make me die as a Muslim, and join me with the righteous.

تَوَفَّنِي مُسْلِمًا وَأَلْحِقْنِي بِالصّٰلِحِينَ

Surah 13

234. 13:8 With Him every thing is by measure.

وَكُلُّ شَيْءٍ عِنْدَهُ بِمِقْدَارٍ

235. 13:9 He is the knower of the unseen (Ghaib) and the visible, the Great, the Lofty.

عٰلِمُ الْغَيْبِ وَالشَّهَادَةِ الْكَبِيرُ الْمُتَعَالِ

236. 13:11 Allah changes not the condition of a folk unless they (first) change that which is in their minds (nafs).

إِنَّ اللّٰهَ لَا يُغَيِّرُ مَا بِقَوْمٍ حَتّٰى يُغَيِّرُوا مَا بِأَنْفُسِهِمْ

237. 13:13 The thunder performs (its part) by His behest and the angels (also) for fear of Him.

وَيُسَبِّحُ الرَّعْدُ بِحَمْدِهِ وَالْمَلٰٓئِكَةُ مِنْ خِيفَتِهِ

238. 13:18 Those who respond to their Lord (Rubb) shall have good (end).

لِلَّذِيْنَ اسْتَجَابُوْا لِرَبِّهِمُ الْحُسْنٰى

239. 13:26 Allah extends provision to whom He pleases and straightens (it for whom He pleases).

اَللّٰهُ يَبْسُطُ الرِّزْقَ لِمَنْ يَّشَآءُ وَيَقْدِرُ

240. 13:29 Blessedness for them and a goodly home (journey's end).

طُوْبٰى لَهُمْ وَحُسْنُ مَاٰبٍ

241. 13:30 Upon Him I rely and to Him I return.

عَلَيْهِ تَوَكَّلْتُ وَاِلَيْهِ مَتَابِ

242. 13:33 He whom Allah suffers to go astray has no guide.

وَمَنْ يُّضْلِلِ اللّٰهُ فَمَا لَهٗ مِنْ هَادٍ

Surah 14

243. 14:7 If you be ungrateful, My torment shall be severe.

وَلَئِنْ كَفَرْتُمْ اِنَّ عَذَابِىْ لَشَدِيْدٌ

244. 14:19 If He pleases, He can remove you away and bring a new creation.

اِنْ يَّشَاْ يُذْهِبْكُمْ وَيَاْتِ بِخَلْقٍ جَدِيْدٍ

245. 15:49 Announce (O Muhammed) to my servants that I am the Forgiving, the Mercy-giving.

نَبِّئْ عِبَادِيٓ أَنِّيٓ أَنَا الْغَفُورُ الرَّحِيمُ

246. 15:56 Who despairs of the mercy of his sustainer (Rubb) except those who go astray?

قَالَ وَمَن يَقْنَطُ مِن رَّحْمَةِ رَبِّهِۦٓ إِلَّا الضَّآلُّونَ

247. 15:86 Your sustainer! (Rubb) He is the Creator, the knowing.

إِنَّ رَبَّكَ هُوَ الْخَلَّٰقُ الْعَلِيمُ

248. 15:88 Droop thy wing (of humility) to the faithful.

وَاخْفِضْ جَنَاحَكَ لِلْمُؤْمِنِينَ

249. 15:94 Proclaim (forcefully) that what you are commanded and turn aside from the idolators.

فَاصْدَعْ بِمَا تُؤْمَرُ وَأَعْرِضْ عَنِ الْمُشْرِكِينَ

250. 15:98 You perform (your part) according to the behests of your sustainer (Rubb) and be of those who worship Him.

فَسَبِّحْ بِحَمْدِ رَبِّكَ وَكُن مِّنَ السَّٰجِدِينَ

251. 15:99 Serve your sustainer (Rubb) until the inevitable (death) comes to you.

وَاعْبُدْ رَبَّكَ حَتَّىٰ يَأْتِيَكَ الْيَقِينُ

Surah 16

252. 16:18 — If you would count the favours of Allah you cannot reckon them.

وَإِن تَعُدُّوا نِعْمَةَ اللَّهِ لَا تُحْصُوهَا

253. 16:52 — His law (Din) is for ever.

وَلَهُ الدِّينُ وَاصِبًا

254. 16:96 — What is with you wastes away (exhausts), but what is with Allah will endure.

مَا عِندَكُمْ يَنفَدُ وَمَا عِندَ اللَّهِ بَاقٍ

255. 16:103 — This (Quran) is in plain Arabic language.

وَهَٰذَا لِسَانٌ عَرَبِيٌّ مُّبِينٌ

Surah 17

256. 17:7 — If you do well,you will do well for your own souls (nafs).

إِنْ أَحْسَنتُمْ أَحْسَنتُمْ لِأَنفُسِكُمْ

257. 17:24 — My Lord! Have compassion on them (both) even as they reared me in childhood.

رَّبِّ ارْحَمْهُمَا كَمَا رَبَّيَانِي صَغِيرًا

258. 17:37 Walk not proudly on the earth .

وَلَا تَمْشِ فِي الْأَرْضِ مَرَحًا

259. 17:57 The torment of thy Lord (Rubb) is to be dreaded.

إِنَّ عَذَابَ رَبِّكَ كَانَ مَحْذُورًا

260. 17:67 Man is ungrateful.

وَكَانَ الْإِنسَانُ كَفُورًا

261. 17:81 Say: Truth has come and falsehood is vanished; verily, falsehood is ever bound to vanish.

وَقُلْ جَاءَ الْحَقُّ وَزَهَقَ الْبَاطِلُ
إِنَّ الْبَاطِلَ كَانَ زَهُوقًا

262. 17:82 We reveal through the Quran that which is a healing and a mercy for the believers.

وَنُنَزِّلُ مِنَ الْقُرْآنِ مَا هُوَ شِفَاءٌ
وَرَحْمَةٌ لِّلْمُؤْمِنِينَ

263. 17:85 No knowledge is given to you except a little.

وَمَا أُوتِيتُم مِّنَ الْعِلْمِ إِلَّا قَلِيلًا

264. 17:100 Man is ever grudging.

وَكَانَ الْإِنسَانُ قَتُورًا

265. 17:105 We have not sent you (O Muhammed) but as a bearer of glad tiding and a warner (bashir and nazir).

وَمَآ اَرْسَلْنٰكَ اِلَّا مُبَشِّرًا وَّنَذِيْرًا

Surah 18

266. 18:5 A grevious is the word that comes out of their mouths.

كَبُرَتْ كَلِمَةً تَخْرُجُ مِنْ اَفْوَاهِهِمْ

267. 18:58 Your sustainer (Rubb) is Forgiving, Mercy-Giving.

وَرَبُّكَ الْغَفُوْرُ ذُو الرَّحْمَةِ

Surah 19

268. 19:36 This is the Straight Path (Sirat-al-Mustaqim).

هٰذَا صِرَاطٌ مُّسْتَقِيْمٌ

Surah 20

269. 20:14 Verily I am Allah. There is no object of worship (Ilah) save Me; so serve Me.

اِنَّنِيْٓ اَنَا اللّٰهُ لَآ اِلٰهَ اِلَّآ اَنَا فَاعْبُدْنِيْ

270. 20:47 Peace will be for him who follows (the right) guidance.

وَالسَّلٰمُ عَلٰى مَنِ اتَّبَعَ الْهُدٰى

271. 20:73 Allah is better and eternal (everlasting).

وَاللّٰهُ خَيْرٌ وَّ اَبْقٰى

272. 20:98 He embrces every thing by His knowledge.

وَسِعَ كُلَّ شَيْءٍ عِلْمًا

273. 20:114 Then exalted be Allah, the king, the truth.

فَتَعٰلَى اللّٰهُ الْمَلِكُ الْحَقُّ

274. 20:114 Say: My Sustainer! (Rubb) increase me in knowledge.

وَقُلْ رَّبِّ زِدْنِيْ عِلْمًا

275. 20:131 The provision of your sustainer (Rubb) is better and eternal (ever lasting).

وَرِزْقُ رَبِّكَ خَيْرٌ وَّ اَبْقٰى

Surah 21

276. 21:1 Their reckoning draws near for mankind.

اِقْتَرَبَ لِلنَّاسِ حِسَابُهُمْ

277. 21:16 We created not the heaven and the earth and all that is between them in sport.

وَمَا خَلَقْنَا السَّمَآءَ وَالْاَرْضَ وَمَا بَيْنَهُمَا لٰعِبِيْنَ

278. 21:20 They glorify (Him) night and day; they faint not.

يُسَبِّحُوْنَ الَّيْلَ وَ النَّهَارَ لَا يَفْتُرُوْنَ

279. 21:47 Though it were but the weight of a grain of mustard seed We would bring it forth (would make account of it).

وَإِنْ كَانَ مِثْقَالَ حَبَّةٍ مِّنْ خَرْدَلٍ أَتَيْنَا بِهَا

280. 21:88 Thus We save the believers.

وَكَذٰلِكَ نُنْجِي الْمُؤْمِنِينَ

281. 21:92 This your Ummah is one Ummah.

إِنَّ هٰذِهٖ أُمَّتُكُمْ أُمَّةً وَّاحِدَةً

283. 21;107 We have not sent you (O muhammed) but as a mercy for all the universe.

وَمَا أَرْسَلْنٰكَ إِلَّا رَحْمَةً لِّلْعٰلَمِينَ

Surah 22

284. 22:10 Allah wrongs not (His servants).

وَأَنَّ اللّٰهَ لَيْسَ بِظَلَّامٍ لِّلْعَبِيدِ

285. 22:11 Losing this world and the hereafter, that is the manifest loss.

خَسِرَ الدُّنْيَا وَالْاٰخِرَةَ ذٰلِكَ هُوَ الْخُسْرَانُ الْمُبِينُ

286. 22:14 Allah does what He intends.

إِنَّ اللّٰهَ يَفْعَلُ مَا يُرِيدُ

287. 22:78 Strife for Allah (with the endeavour) which is its (strife's) due.

وَجَاهِدُوا فِي اللّٰهِ حَقَّ جِهَادِهٖ

Surah 23

288. 23:14 Blessed then be Allah,the best of creators.

فَتَبٰرَكَ اللّٰهُ اَحْسَنُ الْخٰلِقِيْنَ

289. 23:96 Repel evil with that which is better.

اِدْفَعْ بِالَّتِىْ هِىَ اَحْسَنُ السَّيِّئَةَ

290. 23:102 He whose good works are heavy, shall be prosperous (muflihun).

فَمَنْ ثَقُلَتْ مَوَازِيْنُهٗ فَاُولٰٓئِكَ هُمُ الْمُفْلِحُوْنَ

291. 23:115 Did you then think that We had created you in sport and that you will not be returned to Us?

اَفَحَسِبْتُمْ اَنَّمَا خَلَقْنٰكُمْ
عَبَثًا وَّاَنَّكُمْ اِلَيْنَا لَا تُرْجَعُوْنَ

Surah 24

292. 24:10 Had it not been for the Grace of Allah and His Mercy unto you.

وَلَوْلَا فَضْلُ اللّٰهِ عَلَيْكُمْ وَ رَحْمَتُهٗ

293. 24:16 This is awful calumny.

هٰذَا بُهْتَانٌ عَظِيْمٌ

294. 24:21 Allah cleanses whom He pleases.

وَلٰكِنَّ اللّٰهَ يُزَكِّىْ مَنْ يَّشَآءُ

295. 24:31 You who believe turn to Allah (in repentance).

وَتُوبُوٓا إِلَى اللّٰهِ جَمِيعًا أَيُّهَ الْمُؤْمِنُونَ

296. 24:35 Allah is the light of the heavens and the earth.

اَللّٰهُ نُورُ السَّمٰوٰتِ وَالْأَرْضِ

Surah 26

297. 26:9 Thy Lord (Rubb)! He is indeed the Mighty, the Mercy-Giving.

وَإِنَّ رَبَّكَ لَهُوَ الْعَزِيزُ الرَّحِيمُ

298. 26:88 The day when wealth and sons avail not (any man).

يَوْمَ لَا يَنْفَعُ مَالٌ وَّلَا بَنُونَ

299. 26:182 Weigh with true and upright scales.

وَزِنُوا بِالْقِسْطَاسِ الْمُسْتَقِيمِ

300. 26:192 It (the Quran) is a revelation from the sustainer (Rubb) of the universe.

وَإِنَّهُ لَتَنْزِيلُ رَبِّ الْعٰلَمِينَ

301. 26:226 They say what they do not practice.

وَأَنَّهُمْ يَقُولُونَ مَا لَا يَفْعَلُونَ

Surah 27

302. 27:69 Say (O Muhammed) travel in the land and see what was the end of the sinners.

قُلْ سِيرُوا فِي الْأَرْضِ فَانظُرُوا كَيْفَ
كَانَ عَاقِبَةُ الْمُجْرِمِينَ

303. 27:77 It is a guidance and mercy for the believers.

وَإِنَّهُ لَهُدًى وَرَحْمَةٌ لِّلْمُؤْمِنِينَ

304. 27:79 Therefore (O Muhammed!) put thy trust in Allah, for you stand on plain truth.

تَوَكَّلْ عَلَى اللَّهِ إِنَّكَ عَلَى الْحَقِّ الْمُبِينِ

Surah 28

305. 28:21 My sustainer! (Rubb) Save me from the wrong doing people.

الَ رَبِّ نَجِّنِي مِنَ الْقَوْمِ الظَّالِمِينَ

306. 28:60 That which is with Allah is better and eternal.

مَا عِندَ اللَّهِ خَيْرٌ وَأَبْقَىٰ

307. 28:70 His is all praise (obedience) in the first and the last.

الْحَمْدُ فِي الْأُولَىٰ وَالْآخِرَةِ

308. 28:77 Allah loves not those who do mischief (Mufsidin).

إِنَّ اللّٰهَ لَا يُحِبُّ الْمُفْسِدِيْنَ

Surah 29

309. 29:6 Whosoever strives, strives only for his own self (nafs).

وَمَنْ جَاهَدَ فَإِنَّمَا يُجَاهِدُ لِنَفْسِهٖ

310. 29:8 We have enjoined on man, kindness to his parents.

وَوَصَّيْنَا الْاِنْسَانَ بِوَالِدَيْهِ حُسْنًا

311. 29:17 Serve Him and be thankful to Him.

وَاعْبُدُوْهُ وَاشْكُرُوْا لَهٗ

312. 29:43 As for those similitudes, we coin them for men.

وَتِلْكَ الْاَمْثَالُ نَضْرِبُهَا لِلنَّاسِ

313. 29:45 Verily Salat preserves from filthy actions.

اِنَّ الصَّلٰوةَ تَنْهٰى عَنِ الْفَحْشَآءِ وَالْمُنْكَرِ

314. 29:52 Allah is witness enough between me and you.

كَفٰى بِاللّٰهِ بَيْنِيْ وَبَيْنَكُمْ شَهِيْدًا

Surah 30

315. 30:30 Follow Allah's nature (framed by Allah) in which He has created man.

فِطْرَتَ اللّٰهِ الَّتِىْ فَطَرَ النَّاسَ عَلَيْهَا

316. 30:30 There is no change (alteration) in the laws of Allah.

لَا يُخْلِفُ اللّٰهُ وَعْدَهٗ

317. 30:60 Have patience (O Muhammed!) Allah's promise is the only truth.

فَاصْبِرْ اِنَّ وَعْدَ اللّٰهِ حَقٌّ

Surah 31

318. 31:13 Al-Shirk (joining others with Allah) is surely a tremendous wrong.

اِنَّ الشِّرْكَ لَظُلْمٌ عَظِيْمٌ

319. 31:28 Your creation and your resurrection are but as those of one soul.

مَا خَلْقُكُمْ وَلَا بَعْثُكُمْ اِلَّا كَنَفْسٍ وَّاحِدَةٍ

Surah 32

320. 32:7 Who has made every thing good, which He has created.

الَّذِىْٓ اَحْسَنَ كُلَّ شَىْءٍ خَلَقَهٗ

321. 33:4 Allah has not made for a man two hearts within his body.

مَا جَعَلَ اللّٰهُ لِرَجُلٍ مِّنْ قَلْبَيْنِ فِي جَوْفِهِ

322. 33:21 In the messenger of Allah you have a good example.

لَقَدْ كَانَ لَكُمْ فِي رَسُولِ اللّٰهِ أُسْوَةٌ حَسَنَةٌ

323. 33:26 Cast dread (of you) in their hearts.

وَقَذَفَ فِي قُلُوبِهِمُ الرُّعْبَ

324. 33:36 Whosoever disobeys (is rebellious to) Allah and His messengers, goes astray in error manifest.

وَمَنْ يَّعْصِ اللّٰهَ وَرَسُولَهُ فَقَدْ ضَلَّ ضَلٰلًا مُّبِينًا

325. 33:43 He (Allah) is full of mercy to His believers.

إِنَّا كَذٰلِكَ نَجْزِي الْمُحْسِنِينَ

326. 33:71 Whosoever obeys Allah and His messenger has attained a great (signal) victory.

وَمَنْ يُّطِعِ اللّٰهَ وَرَسُولَهُ فَقَدْ فَازَ فَوْزًا عَظِيمًا

327. 33:72 He has proved a tyrant and ignorant.

إِنَّهُ كَانَ ظَلُومًا جَهُولًا

Surah 34

328. 34:28 We have not sent you (O Muhammed!) save as bearer of glad tidings and as warner to mankind.

وَمَآ اَرْسَلْنٰكَ اِلَّا كَآفَّةً لِّلنَّاسِ بَشِيْرًا وَّنَذِيْرًا

Surah 35

329. 35:1 Praise (obedience) be to Allah, the creator of the heavens and the earth.

اَلْحَمْدُ لِلّٰهِ فَاطِرِ السَّمٰوٰتِ وَالْاَرْضِ

Surah 36

330. 36:17 Upon us (prophet devolves) nothing but plain conveyance (of the message).

وَمَا عَلَيْنَآ اِلَّا الْبَلٰغُ الْمُبِيْنُ

331. 36:69 We have not taught him (Muhammed) poetry nor was it befitting him.

وَمَا عَلَّمْنٰهُ الشِّعْرَ وَمَا يَنْۢبَغِيْ لَهٗ

Surah 37

332. 37:4 Thy Lord (Ilah) is surely one.

اِنَّ اِلٰهَكُمْ لَوَاحِدٌ

333. 37:35 There is no god except Allah.

لَآ إِلَٰهَ إِلَّا ٱللَّهُ

334. 37:180 Thy Lord (rubb) the Lord of Honour and Power is above of what they ascribe(to Him).

سُبْحَٰنَ رَبِّكَ رَبِّ ٱلْعِزَّةِ عَمَّا يَصِفُونَ

Surah 38

335. 38:65 There is no god but Allah, the One, the Dominant.

وَمَا مِنْ إِلَٰهٍ إِلَّا ٱللَّهُ ٱلْوَٰحِدُ ٱلْقَهَّارُ

Surah 39

336. 39:9 Only men of understanding will pay heed

إِنَّمَا يَتَذَكَّرُ أُولُوا۟ ٱلْأَلْبَٰبِ

337. 39:20 (This is the) promise of Allah. Allah fails not His promise.

وَعْدَ ٱللَّهِ لَا يُخْلِفُ ٱللَّهُ ٱلْمِيعَادَ

338. 39:26 Surely the torment of the hereafter shall be greater still; did they but know.

وَلَعَذَابُ ٱلْءَاخِرَةِ أَكْبَرُ لَوْ كَانُوا۟ يَعْلَمُونَ

339. 39:36 Is not Allah sufficient for His servant?

أَلَيْسَ ٱللَّهُ بِكَافٍ عَبْدَهُۥ

340. 39:44 Say: Unto Allah belongs all intercession.

قُلْ لِّلّٰهِ الشَّفَاعَةُ جَمِيْعًا

341. 39:53 Despair not of the mercy of Allah.

لَا تَقْنَطُوْا مِنْ رَّحْمَةِ اللّٰهِ

Surah 40

342. 40:7 O my lord (Rubb) You embrace all things in mercy and knowledge.

رَبَّنَا وَسِعْتَ كُلَّ شَيْءٍ رَّحْمَةً وَّعِلْمًا

343. 40:9 That is the supreme triumph.

وَذٰلِكَ هُوَ الْفَوْزُ الْعَظِيْمُ

344. 40:16 Whose is the sovereignty this day? It is of Allah, the One, the Dominant.

لِمَنِ الْمُلْكُ الْيَوْمَ ۭ لِلّٰهِ الْوَاحِدِ الْقَهَّارِ

345. 40:17 Today shall every soul be rewarded for what it has earned (of good or evil).

اَلْيَوْمَ تُجْزٰى كُلُّ نَفْسٍ بِمَا كَسَبَتْ

346. 40:31 Allah desires not wrong to His servants.

وَمَا اللّٰهُ يُرِيْدُ ظُلْمًا لِّلْعِبَادِ

347. 40:44 I commit my affair to Allah.

وَاُفَوِّضُ اَمْرِيْٓ اِلَى اللّٰهِ

348. 40:56 (You) take refuge in Allah.

فَاسْتَعِذْ بِاللّٰهِ

349. 40:58 The blind and the seer are not equal.

وَمَا يَسْتَوِى الْاَعْمٰى وَالْبَصِيْرُ

Surah 41

350. 41:49 Man is not tired of praying for good and if ill touches him, then he is disheartened, desperate.

لَا يَسْئَمُ الْاِنْسَانُ مِنْ دُعَاءِ الْخَيْرِ

وَاِنْ مَّسَّهُ الشَّرُّ فَيَئُوْسٌ قَنُوْطٌ

Surah 42

351. 42:11 Nothing is like Him.

لَيْسَ كَمِثْلِهٖ شَيْءٌ

352. 42:15 Allah is our Lord (Rubb) and also yours.

اَللّٰهُ رَبُّنَا وَرَبُّكُمْ

353. 42:15 To us our deeds and to you, your deeds.

لَنَآ اَعْمَالُنَا وَلَكُمْ اَعْمَالُكُمْ

354. 42:22 This is the great preferment.

ذٰلِكَ هُوَ الْفَضْلُ الْكَبِيْرُ

355. 42:25 It is He who accepts repentance.

وَهُوَ الَّذِىْ يَقْبَلُ التَّوْبَةَ عَنْ عِبَادِهٖ

356. 42:31 Beside Allah there is no protecting friend or any helper for you.

وَمَا لَكُم مِّن دُونِ اللَّهِ مِن وَلِيٍّ وَلَا نَصِيرٍ

357. 42:38 Whose affairs are a matter of counsel

وَأَمْرُهُمْ شُورَىٰ بَيْنَهُمْ

358. 42:38 Who spend of what we have bestowed on them.

وَمِمَّا رَزَقْنَٰهُمْ يُنفِقُونَ

359. 42:40 The recompense of evil is punishment like it.

وَجَزَٰٓؤُا سَيِّئَةٍ سَيِّئَةٌ مِّثْلُهَا

360. 42:50 He is Knowing; Powerful.

إِنَّهُۥ عَلِيمٌ قَدِيرٌ

Surah 45

361. 45:3 In the heavens and the earth there are signs for the believers.

إِنَّ فِي السَّمَٰوَٰتِ وَالْأَرْضِ لَءَايَٰتٍ لِّلْمُؤْمِنِينَ

362. 45:22 Allah created the heavens and the earth with truth.

وَخَلَقَ اللَّهُ السَّمَٰوَٰتِ وَالْأَرْضَ بِالْحَقِّ

363. 45:29 This our book will speak concerning you with truth.

هَٰذَا كِتَٰبُنَا يَنطِقُ عَلَيْكُم بِالْحَقِّ

364. 45:37 His the greatness in the heavens and the earth.

وَلَهُ الْكِبْرِيَآءُ فِي السَّمٰوٰتِ وَ الْاَرْضِ

Surah 46

365. 46:21 I fear for you the torment of a great day.

اِنِّيْٓ اَخَافُ عَلَيْكُمْ عَذَابَ يَوْمٍ عَظِيْمٍ

366. 46:30 Guiding to the truth and to the straight way.

يَهْدِيْٓ اِلَى الْحَقِّ وَاِلٰى طَرِيْقٍ مُّسْتَقِيْمٍ

Surah 47

367. 47:3 Thus Allah coins (strikes out) similitudes for you.

كَذٰلِكَ يَضْرِبُ اللّٰهُ لِلنَّاسِ اَمْثَالَهُمْ

368. 47:11 The disbelievers have no patron.

وَاَنَّ الْكٰفِرِيْنَ لَا مَوْلٰى لَهُمْ

369. 47:24 Will they then not mediate on the Quran, or are there locks on their hearts?

اَفَلَا يَتَدَبَّرُوْنَ الْقُرْاٰنَ اَمْ عَلٰى قُلُوْبٍ اَقْفَالُهَا

370. 47:35 Allah is with you.

وَاللّٰهُ مَعَكُمْ

371. 47:38 If you turn away He will bring in your stead a people other than you and they shall not be like you.

وَإِن تَتَوَلَّوْا يَسْتَبْدِلْ قَوْمًا غَيْرَكُمْ
ثُمَّ لَا يَكُونُوٓا أَمْثَالَكُم

Surah 48

372. 48:1 We have given you a manifest victory.

إِنَّا فَتَحْنَا لَكَ فَتْحًا مُّبِينًا

373. 48:3 That Allah may help you with a mighty help.

وَيَنصُرَكَ اللَّهُ نَصْرًا عَزِيزًا

374. 48:11 They speak with their tongues what is not in their hearts.

يَقُولُونَ بِأَلْسِنَتِهِم مَّا لَيْسَ فِي قُلُوبِهِمْ

375. 48:28 That He may show it (Islam) above all religions (din).

لِيُظْهِرَهُۥ عَلَى الدِّينِ كُلِّهِۦ

376. 48:29 Muhammed the messenger of Allah and those with him are hard against the disbelievers and merciful among themselves.

مُّحَمَّدٌ رَّسُولُ اللَّهِ وَالَّذِينَ مَعَهُۥٓ أَشِدَّآءُ
عَلَى الْكُفَّارِ رُحَمَآءُ بَيْنَهُمْ

Surah 49

377. 49:8 As a grace from Allah and (His) favour.

فَضْلًا مِّنَ اللّٰهِ وَ نِعْمَةً

378. 49:9 Allah loves those who act fairly.

إِنَّ اللّٰهَ يُحِبُّ الْمُقْسِطِيْنَ

379. 49:11 Neither defame one another nor insult one another.

وَلَا تَلْمِزُوْٓا أَنْفُسَكُمْ وَلَا تَنَابَزُوْا بِالْأَلْقَابِ

380. 49:13 Noblest (most honorable) of you in the sight of Allah is he who is pious (best in conduct).

إِنَّ أَكْرَمَكُمْ عِنْدَ اللّٰهِ أَتْقٰىكُمْ

Surah 50

381. 50:16 We are nearer to him than his jugular vein.

وَنَحْنُ أَقْرَبُ إِلَيْهِ مِنْ حَبْلِ الْوَرِيْدِ

Surah 51

382. 51:6 The (day of) Judgement will surely come.

وَّإِنَّ الدِّيْنَ لَوَاقِعٌ

383. 51:19 In their wealth there is a right for the beggar (who asks) and the person who did not ask.

وَفِيْٓ أَمْوَالِهِمْ حَقٌّ لِّلسَّآئِلِ وَالْمَحْرُوْمِ

384. 51:55 Remind (them of their duties); for verily the reminder shall profit the believers.

وَذَكِّرْ فَإِنَّ الذِّكْرَىٰ تَنفَعُ الْمُؤْمِنِينَ

Surah 52

385. 52:48 Crlebrate the praise of your sustainer (Rubb) any time (of the night) you rise up.

وَسَبِّحْ بِحَمْدِ رَبِّكَ حِينَ تَقُومُ

Surah 53

386. 53:3 Nor does he (the prophet) speak of (his own selfish) desire.

وَمَا يَنطِقُ عَنِ الْهَوَىٰ

387. 53:9 So that he became (as though he were) one single grip of the two bows (of the archers, in vowing feality to each other) or closer still.

فَكَانَ قَابَ قَوْسَيْنِ أَوْ أَدْنَىٰ

388. 53:17 The eye turned not aside nor it was overbold.

مَا زَاغَ الْبَصَرُ وَمَا طَغَىٰ

389. 53:23 Now the guidance from their Lord (Rubb) has come to them.

وَلَقَدْ جَاءَهُم مِّن رَّبِّهِمُ الْهُدَىٰ

390. 53:39 That man shall have nothing other than what he strives for.

وَأَنْ لَّيْسَ لِلْإِنْسَانِ إِلَّا مَا سَعٰى

391. 53:55 Concerning which then, of the bounties of your Lord (Rubb) can you dispute (O man!).

فَبِأَيِّ آلَاءِ رَبِّكَ تَتَمَارٰى

Surah 54

392. 54:17 In truth We have made the Quran, easy for reminding; but is there any who is (willing to be) reminded?

وَلَقَدْ يَسَّرْنَا الْقُرْاٰنَ لِلذِّكْرِ فَهَلْ مِنْ مُّدَّكِرٍ

Surah 55

393. 55:26 Every thing (in the universe) shall face extinction.

كُلُّ مَنْ عَلَيْهَا فَانٍ

394. 55:60 Is the reward of goodness (ihsan) any other than goodness (ihsan).

هَلْ جَزَآءُ الْإِحْسَانِ إِلَّا الْإِحْسَانُ

Surah 56

395. 56:79 None touches (or will touch) it (the Quran) except the clean (at heart).

لَا يَمَسُّهٗٓ إِلَّا الْمُطَهَّرُوْنَ

396. 56:96 Therefore (O Muhammed) praise the name of your Lord (Rubb), the Tremendous.

فَسَبِّحْ بِاسْمِ رَبِّكَ الْعَظِيمِ

Surah 57

397. 57:4 He (Allah) is with you wherever you are.

وَهُوَ مَعَكُمْ أَيْنَ مَا كُنتُمْ

398. 57:4 Allah sees what you do.

وَاللَّهُ بِمَا تَعْمَلُونَ بَصِيرٌ

399. 57:20 Pardon from Allah and His pleasure.

وَمَغْفِرَةٌ مِّنَ اللَّهِ وَرِضْوَانٌ

400. 57:21 That is the grace of Allah which He gives to whom He pleases and Allah is full of great grace.

ذَٰلِكَ فَضْلُ اللَّهِ يُؤْتِيهِ مَن يَشَاءُ
وَاللَّهُ ذُو الْفَضْلِ الْعَظِيمِ

Surah 58

401. 58:5 (They) shall be brought low as those before them were brought low.

كُبِتُوا كَمَا كُبِتَ الَّذِينَ مِن قَبْلِهِمْ

402. 58:22 This is the party of Allah; is it not the party which will attain success?

أُولَٰٓئِكَ حِزْبُ ٱللَّهِ ۚ أَلَآ إِنَّ حِزْبَ ٱللَّهِ هُمُ ٱلْمُفْلِحُونَ

Surah 59

403. 59:2 Allah came upon them from whence they did not expect.

فَأَتَىٰهُمُ ٱللَّهُ مِنْ حَيْثُ لَمْ يَحْتَسِبُوا۟

404. 59:14 They are a people who have no sense.

ذَٰلِكَ بِأَنَّهُمْ قَوْمٌ لَّا يَعْقِلُونَ

405. 59:22 He (Allah) is the knower of the unseen and the visible. He is the Merciful, the Mercy-Giving.

عَٰلِمُ ٱلْغَيْبِ وَٱلشَّهَٰدَةِ ۖ هُوَ ٱلرَّحْمَٰنُ ٱلرَّحِيمُ

Surah 60

406. 60:3 Your kinship shall by no means benefit you nor your children on the day of resurrection.

لَن تَنفَعَكُمْ أَرْحَامُكُمْ وَلَآ أَوْلَٰدُكُمْ ۚ يَوْمَ ٱلْقِيَٰمَةِ

407. 60:4 Our Lord!(Rubb)upon You we rely and to You we turn and to You (our) journey (ends).

رَّبَّنَا عَلَيْكَ تَوَكَّلْنَا وَإِلَيْكَ أَنَبْنَا
وَإِلَيْكَ ٱلْمَصِيرُ

408. 60:5 Our Lord! (Rubb} Make us not a prey (trial) for those who disbelieve (kafirun).

رَبَّنَا لَا تَجْعَلْنَا فِتْنَةً لِّلَّذِينَ كَفَرُوا

409. 60:13 O Believers! Take not for patrons a people against whom Allah is angered.

يَٰٓأَيُّهَا الَّذِينَ ءَامَنُوا لَا تَتَوَلَّوْا قَوْمًا غَضِبَ اللَّهُ عَلَيْهِمْ

Surah 61

410. 61:13 Help from Allah and the victory (which is) near.

نَصْرٌ مِّنَ اللَّهِ وَفَتْحٌ قَرِيبٌ

Surah 62

411. 62:11 What is with Allah is better than pastime (sport) and merchandise.

قُلْ مَا عِندَ اللَّهِ خَيْرٌ مِّنَ اللَّهْوِ وَمِنَ التِّجَارَةِ

412. 62:11 Allah is the best of the providers.

وَاللَّهُ خَيْرُ الرَّٰزِقِينَ

Surah 64

413. 64:4 Allah is aware of what is in the breasts (of men).

وَاللَّهُ عَلِيمٌ بِذَاتِ الصُّدُورِ

414. 64:11 No calamity befalls save by Allah's leave.

مَآ اَصَابَ مِنْ مُّصِيْبَةٍ اِلَّا بِاِذْنِ اللّٰهِ

415. 64:11 Whosoever believes in Allah, He guides his heart.

وَمَنْ يُّؤْمِنْ بِاللّٰهِ يَهْدِ قَلْبَهٗ

Surah 65

416. 65:1 Whoso transgresses the bounds of Allah has wronged himself.

وَمَنْ يَّتَعَدَّ حُدُوْدَ اللّٰهِ فَقَدْ ظَلَمَ نَفْسَهٗ

417. 65:2 Stand fast (to truth) in bearing witness before Allah.

وَ اَقِيْمُوا الشَّهَادَةَ لِلّٰهِ

418. 65:2 Whoso fears Allah He will make for him a way out (of all difficulties).

وَمَنْ يَّتَّقِ اللّٰهَ يَجْعَلْ لَّهٗ مَخْرَجًا

419. 65:3 He will provide for him from whence he expects (it) not.

وَّيَرْزُقْهُ مِنْ حَيْثُ لَا يَحْتَسِبُ

420. 65:11 Allah has made a goodly provision for him.

قَدْ اَحْسَنَ اللّٰهُ لَهٗ رِزْقًا

Surah 66

421. 66:8 — O Believers! Turn to Allah with sincere repentance.

يَآاَيُّهَا الَّذِيْنَ اٰمَنُوْا تُوْبُوْآ
اِلَى اللّٰهِ تَوْبَةً نَّصُوْحًا

Surah 68

422. 68:4 — (O Muhammed!) You are on a grand (level of) character.

وَاِنَّكَ لَعَلٰى خُلُقٍ عَظِيْمٍ

Surah 69

423. 69:24 — Eat and drink with healthy relish (as a reward) for what you have sent on before (you) in the days which are past.

كُلُوْا وَاشْرَبُوْا هَنِيْٓـًٔا بِمَآ اَسْلَفْتُمْ فِى
الْاَيَّامِ الْخَالِيَةِ

424. 69:48 — Verily it (the Quran) is a reminder to those who fear (to do wrong).

وَاِنَّهٗ لَتَذْكِرَةٌ لِّلْمُتَّقِيْنَ

Surah 70

425. 70:19 Man is created impatient.

إِنَّ الْإِنسَانَ خُلِقَ هَلُوعًا

Surah 71

426. 71:10 Seek pardon of your Lord (Rubb) Lo! He is ever forgiving.

اسْتَغْفِرُوا رَبَّكُمْ إِنَّهُ كَانَ غَفَّارًا

427. 71:15 Do not see how Allah created seven planets moving in harmony with one another.

أَلَمْ تَرَوْا كَيْفَ خَلَقَ اللَّهُ سَبْعَ سَمٰوٰتٍ طِبَاقًا

Surah 73

428. 73:4 Read the the Quran in measured tone.

وَرَتِّلِ الْقُرْاٰنَ تَرْتِيلًا

429. 73:10 Bear with patience what they utter.

وَاصْبِرْ عَلَىٰ مَا يَقُولُونَ

430. 73:17 How then shall you protect yourself if you deny (Allah) on the Day that will turn children grey?

فَكَيْفَ تَتَّقُونَ إِن كَفَرْتُمْ يَوْمًا

يَجْعَلُ الْوِلْدَانَ شِيبًا

431. 73:18 His (Allah's) promise shall surely be accomplished.

كَانَ وَعْدُهُ مَفْعُولًا

432. 73:19 This (Quran) is a reminder:let him then who wills, take the way of his Lord (Rubb).

إِنَّ هٰذِهِ تَذْكِرَةٌ فَمَنْ شَآءَ اتَّخَذَ إِلَىٰ رَبِّهِ سَبِيلًا

Surah 75

433. 75:17 Upon Us is the collecting thereof and the proclamation thereof.

إِنَّ عَلَيْنَا جَمْعَهُ وَقُرْاٰنَهُ

Surah 76

434. 76:30 Please you shall not, unless Allah pleases.

وَمَا تَشَآءُونَ إِلَّآ أَنْ يَّشَآءَ اللّٰهُ

Surah 77

435. 77:49 Woe on that Day, to those who call (it) a lie.

وَيْلٌ يَّوْمَئِذٍ لِّلْمُكَذِّبِيْنَ

Surah 78

436. 78:8 We created you in pairs.

وَخَلَقْنٰكُمْ أَزْوَاجًا

437. 78:11 Made the day for (gaining) livelihood.

وَجَعَلْنَا النَّهَارَ مَعَاشًا

Surah 81

438. 81:14 The soul shall know what is has brought forth.

عَلِمَتْ نَفْسٌ مَّآ أَحْضَرَتْ

439. 81:27 It is a reminder to all the world.

إِنْ هُوَ إِلَّا ذِكْرٌ لِّلْعٰلَمِينَ

Surah 82

440. 82:13 The righteous shall be in delight.

إِنَّ الْأَبْرَارَ لَفِي نَعِيمٍ

Surah 83

441. 83:1 Woe to those who tilt the measure.

وَيْلٌ لِّلْمُطَفِّفِينَ

Surah 85

442. 85:12 Verily, the grip of your Lord (Rubb) is severe.

إِنَّ بَطْشَ رَبِّكَ لَشَدِيدٌ

Surah 86

443. 86:4 There is no soul but it has a guardian (set) over it.

إِن كُلُّ نَفْسٍ لَّمَّا عَلَيْهَا حَافِظٌ

Surah 87

444. 87:14 Now shall he prosper who clears himself.

قَدْ أَفْلَحَ مَن تَزَكَّىٰ

Surah 88

445. 88:21 Remind (them O Muhammed!) you are only to remind; you have no authority over them.

فَذَكِّرْ إِنَّمَا أَنتَ مُذَكِّرٌ لَّسْتَ عَلَيْهِم بِمُصَيْطِرٍ

Surah 89

446. 89:17 Ay! but you honour not the orphan.

كَلَّا بَل لَّا تُكْرِمُونَ الْيَتِيمَ

447. 89:18 Nor stir up (others) to feed the poor.

وَلَا تَحٰٓضُّوْنَ عَلٰى طَعَامِ الْمِسْكِيْنِ

448. 89:19 You devour the inheritance, devouring greedily.

وَتَاْكُلُوْنَ التُّرَاثَ اَكْلًا لَّمًّا

449. 89:20 You love wealth with exceeding love.

وَّتُحِبُّوْنَ الْمَالَ حُبًّا جَمًّا

450. 89:29 Enter you among My devotees.

فَادْخُلِيْ فِيْ عِبٰدِيْ

Surah 90

451. 90:4 We have certainly created man in (an atmosphere of) toil.

لَقَدْ خَلَقْنَا الْاِنْسَانَ فِيْ كَبَدٍ

Surah 92

452. 92:7 We will certainly speed him onward to ease.

وَصَدَّقَ بِالْحُسْنٰى

Surah 93

453. 93:10 As to him who asks chide(him)not away.

وَاَمَّا السَّآئِلَ فَلَا تَنْهَرْ

Surah 94

454. 94:4 Raised for you your reputation.

وَرَفَعْنَا لَكَ ذِكْرَكَ

455. 94:5 Then verily with trouble (comes) ease.

فَإِنَّ مَعَ الْعُسْرِ يُسْرًا

Surah 95

456. 95:4 We have certainly created man in the best of structures.

لَقَدْ خَلَقْنَا الْإِنْسَانَ فِي أَحْسَنِ تَقْوِيمٍ

Surah 96

457. 96:5 (Thereby) Taught man what (otherwise) he would not know.

عَلَّمَ الْإِنْسَانَ مَا لَمْ يَعْلَمْ

Surah 98

458. 98:5 To establish worship (Salat) and to pay alms (Zakat) that is the true (standard) religion (Din).

وَيُقِيمُوا الصَّلٰوةَ وَيُؤْتُوا الزَّكٰوةَ وَذٰلِكَ دِينُ الْقَيِّمَةِ

Surah 99

459. 99:7 Whoso does good an atom's weight, will then see it.

فَمَن يَعْمَلْ مِثْقَالَ ذَرَّةٍ خَيْرًا يَرَهُ

Surah 100

460. 100:6 Verily man is ungrateful to his Lord (Rubb).

إِنَّ الْإِنسَانَ لِرَبِّهِ لَكَنُودٌ

Surah 103

461. 103:2 Verily man is in a state of loss.

إِنَّ الْإِنسَانَ لَفِي خُسْرٍ

462. 103:3 Enjoin truth (on each other) and enjoin endurance (steadfastness, on each other).

وَتَوَاصَوْا بِالْحَقِّ وَتَوَاصَوْا بِالصَّبْرِ

Surah 107

463. 107:4 Woe to worshippers (Mussalis) who are careless in prayers (Salat).

فَوَيْلٌ لِّلْمُصَلِّينَ ۝٤
الَّذِينَ هُمْ عَن صَلَاتِهِمْ سَاهُونَ

Surah 108

464. 108:1 We have given you (O Muhammed) good (in) abundance.

اِنَّآ اَعْطَيْنٰكَ الْكَوْثَرَ

Surah 109

465. 109:6 You have your religion (Din) and I have my religion (Din).

لَكُمْ دِيْنُكُمْ وَلِيَ دِيْنِ

Surah 110

466. 110:3 Then hymn the praises of your Sustainer (Rubb) and seek His forgiveness.

فَسَبِّحْ بِحَمْدِ رَبِّكَ وَاسْتَغْفِرْهُ

Surah 111

467. 111:2 His wealth shall not avail him nor what he earns.

مَآ اَغْنٰى عَنْهُ مَالُهٗ وَمَا كَسَبَ